Jonathan C. Erwin

# The
# Classroom
# of Choice

Giving Students
What They Need
and Getting
What You Want

Association for Supervision and
Curriculum Development
Alexandria, Virginia USA

Association for Supervision and Curriculum Development
1703 N. Beauregard St. Alexandria, VA 22311-1714 USA
Telephone: 800-933-2723 or 703-578-9600 Fax: 703-575-5400
Web site: http://www.ascd.org E-mail: member@ascd.org

Gene R. Carter, *Executive Director*; Nancy Modrak, *Director of Publishing*; Julie Houtz, *Director of Book Editing & Production*; Tim Sniffin, *Project Manager*; Georgia McDonald, *Senior Graphic Designer*; Jim Beals, *Typesetter*; Dina Murray Seamon, *Production Specialist*.

ASCD Member Book, No. FY04-7 (May 2004, P). ASCD Member Books mail to Premium (P), Comprehensive(C), and Regular (R) members on this schedule: Jan., PC; Feb., P; Apr., PCR; May, P; July, PC; Aug., P; Sept., PCR; Nov., PC; Dec., P.

Paperback ISBN: 0-87120-829-6 • ASCD product #104020
List Price: $26.95 ($21.95 ASCD member price, direct from ASCD only)

e-books ($26.95): netLibrary ISBN 0-87120-997-7 ebrary ISBN 0-87120-998-5


**Library of Congress Cataloging-in-Publication Data**
Erwin, Jonathan C., 1954-
  The classroom of choice : giving students what they need and getting what you want / Jonathan C. Erwin.
    p. cm.
  Includes bibliographical references and index.
  ISBN 0-87120-829-6 (alk. paper) — ISBN 0-87120-997-7 (e-book netlibrary) — ISBN 0-87120-998-5 (e-book ebrary)
  1. Classroom management. 2. Motivation in education. I. Title.

  LB3013.E73 2004
  371.102'4—dc22

                    2004001824

10 09 08 07 06 05 04        12 11 10 9 8 7 6 5 4 3 2 1

*To Russell L. Erwin and Kathryn R. Erwin*

*Loving parents and inspiring teachers*

# The Classroom of Choice

Giving Students
What They Need
and Getting
What You Want

# Acknowledgments

Valuable human accomplishments are never the work of one individual; they are based on the combined efforts of many others over many years. I would like to thank the following people for their part in the creation of this book:

- To Nancy Erwin and my son Nate for their encouragement.
- To William Glasser for his life's work dedicated to the improvement of education and mental health.
- To my friend, colleague, and mentor Robert Sullo for his inspiration, useful feedback, and constant encouragement.
- To all the faculty members and staff of The William Glasser Institute for sharing their knowledge and skills and for their inspiration, particularly Al Katz, Peter Appel, Nancy Buck, Bob Wubbolding, Linda Harshman, Shelley Punzo, Lynn Sumida, Kathy Curtis, Pat Robey, Bob Hoglund, Kim Olver, and Rolf Ahrens.
- To all the other members of The William Glasser Institute and Quality School Consortium.
- To all my former students for teaching me the importance of good student-teacher relationships.
- To all the dedicated teachers I've worked with over the years.

# Foreword

FOR WHOM IS *THE CLASSROOM OF CHOICE?* IF YOU HAVE EVER EXPRESSED ONE or more of the following goals for your students, then this book is for you!

- I want to inspire young people to do their best.
- I want my students to learn what they need to be responsible members of society.
- I want young people to respect each other and themselves.
- I want to help students achieve their potential.
- I want my students to be thinkers and problem solvers.
- I want students to love learning.
- I want my students to be independent.
- I want my students to live happy and healthy lives.
- I want young people to be motivated to excel in . . . (math, science, English, art, music, drama, athletics, and so on).
- I just want my students to be successful in my class (or organization).

Although primarily designed with teachers in mind, this book offers many useful management and instructional tips to anyone who works with young people: coaches, church youth group leaders, play directors, club advisors, and so forth. It provides hundreds of specific strategies you can use with young people to appeal to what intrinsically motivates them in order for high-quality learning to take place. It is about giving kids what they need, and in doing so, getting what you want. It is about creating the classroom of choice.

## How to Use *The Classroom of Choice*

Here are just a couple ways you might consider using this book:

- *As a toolbox.* This book can be used as a resource for those of you who simply want to add to the teaching and management strategies that are already working for you. You might want to use a new team-building activity, offer your students a choice of performance assessments, or add some novelty to your classroom. Just select from the strategies explained in the following chapters to add one or more tools to your personal toolbox.

- *As a planning guide.* The book also provides a simple unit guide that can easily be combined with, or superimposed over, any planning approach your school or district may have adopted. The unit guide, which I call "I-Five," divides the learning cycle into four phases: Introduction, Instruction, Integration, and Implementation. All four of these phases of the human learning cycle happen within the fifth "I," the circle of Involvement, which has to do with creating an optimal learning environment. Within the involvement circle and each of the four phases, we can appeal to students' intrinsic motivation by providing specific opportunities for students to meet their five basic needs. The greatest benefit of using this approach is its intentionality. We can develop and manage our learning environment by chance or by choice. Using the planning guide is one way of being intentional about what you do to get what you want in your classroom.

However you decide to use this book, remember this: You are the expert in your grade level and subject. You will know which strategies will work best for your students. I intentionally did not categorize activities into grade levels because often an activity that seems to be too young for secondary students or too mature for elementary students might become an effective and enjoyable teaching strategy with minor adaptation. Through the years I've spent in staff development, I've learned how innovative teachers are. I'd invite you as you read to consider ways you could use or modify these strategies for your subject area and your students' developmental ability. Intentionally and appropriately implemented, the strategies in this book will help you make your classroom a joyful place: a classroom of choice!

# Introduction

"DON'T SMILE UNTIL THANKSGIVING!"

That was the advice I most remember from my undergraduate Methods of Teaching Secondary English course. I was in trouble before I even entered the classroom. I knew I wouldn't be able to heed that advice for long. I was right. As soon as my first class of 7th graders came into my classroom, with every book they had precariously crammed under one arm and a look on their faces that could only be described as equal parts eagerness and fear, I blew it: I smiled. I should have known right then that the traditional classroom management practices I'd been taught would be just as useless as the advice not to smile. But, not knowing any other way, I used them: a combination of positive reinforcement and, on occasion, punishment. My teaching strategies were equally traditional. The results? They were okay. Academically, my students fell into the normal distribution pattern of the old bell curve: A few students excelled, a few failed, and the vast majority fell into the average C range. Behaviorally, it was similar. I had a few model students, a few chronic behavior problems, but most were acceptable—behaving responsibly as long as I remained vigilant.

"Is this it?" I asked myself. Is this why I entered teaching, to spend the next 30 years monitoring behavior while accepting mediocre learning and performance from my students? Of course not! I wanted to have great relationships with my students. I wanted to inspire them. But I didn't know how. Then one summer, I was invited to take a workshop, a Basic Intensive Week in Choice Theory. "Why not?" I asked myself. "It pays a pretty good stipend." Surprisingly, it was, for me, the week that changed my life. This was the stuff I needed to hear in my education classes in college.

I couldn't wait to implement these new ideas in my classroom in September. But, having been to a number of other workshops and having had mixed results at best when trying to apply the ideas, I was a little skeptical about what would happen when I tried to utilize Choice Theory. This time it was different. I'm not saying that my classroom was transformed overnight, but little by little, intentionally applying these ideas to my teaching and managing style, my classroom became the place I had always hoped it would be. Behavior problems all but disappeared, and my students' learning and performance improved dramatically. Instead of the old bell-shaped curve, now I had more of a J-shaped curve: almost all students achieving in the A and B range. Most important, my classroom became a joyful place for both my students and me.

While still teaching, I was asked to lead in-service workshops in Choice Theory for teachers in my district. I gained so much satisfaction from teaching these ideas to my colleagues, who also were finding them valuable, that when a staff development position that specified knowledge of Choice Theory opened at the local Board of Cooperative Educational Services in New York State, I jumped at the opportunity. It was difficult leaving my classroom, but since taking the position, I have thoroughly enjoyed helping teachers achieve more of what they want in their classrooms. Also, I continue to learn new ways of implementing Choice Theory concepts that I only wish I had known when I was still teaching middle and high school English students.

This book is about teaching, but it is really more about learning. Therefore, I begin this book by asking you to think about a learning experience of your own. Think of something you recently learned where you faced a steep learning curve. In other words, think of something you learned that did not come easily. Your learning example could be academic in nature, such as a graduate or continuing education course. It might be a hobby, such learning to play golf, to quilt, or to sail. Your learning might have to do with a change in lifestyle, such as learning to integrate an exercise program into your life or to quit smoking. Maybe your learning situation has something to do with a new relationship: learning to be a son- or daughter-in-law, to be married, or to be a parent. Or maybe your learning is related to improving your skills as a teacher: learning to integrate technology into the classroom or to appeal to multiple intelligences.

Now, think of the feelings you had during this learning experience. It's likely that at certain times during your learning, you felt frustration, impatience, embarrassment, fear, anger, self-doubt, hopelessness, or other painful emotions. At other points, you probably felt encouragement, satisfaction, confidence, fulfillment, pride, and other pleasurable emotions. On any learning journey, we experience both highs and lows until at some point we satisfy our learning objective.

As a teacher, learning never stops. Teaching *is* learning. It involves, among other things, learning to manage a classroom of students, learning to teach students with different learning styles, learning to provide an environment where children are intrinsically motivated to do their best, learning to contend with mountains of paperwork, all the while learning to balance one's personal and professional life. For teachers, the highs and lows of the learning journey never stop. And if what the French philosopher Joseph Joubert said is true, that "teaching is twice learning," then it would make sense that teachers experience twice the fulfillment and twice the frustration of the average learner. In my years of experience leading staff development workshops for educators, I have heard hundreds of teachers tell about both sides of the teaching-learning experience, the peak moments of satisfaction and the low points of frustration and anger. I agree with Joubert. Teaching is simultaneously the most satisfying and most challenging profession there is. The purpose of this book is to help teachers experience more moments of joy and fulfillment and fewer moments of frustration and stress.

The first step toward a more satisfying teaching experience is to understand that the students in our classrooms are like us. Their learning experience involves a ride on an emotional roller coaster. Some students hide their feelings, and it is difficult to assess whether they are experiencing pleasurable or painful feelings. With others, there is no doubt. The pleasant feelings are easy to contend with. It is when students are angry, frustrated, or hopeless and act out these feelings in inappropriate and irresponsible ways that they create frustrating and stressful situations for us. Therefore, if teachers can reduce the amount of time students experience anger, frustration, and so forth, they will simultaneously reduce their own painful feelings.

This book will focus on a new classroom management model that aligns itself with what truly motivates human behavior. It's about providing students with what they truly need so that teachers can get more of what they want. The result of implementing this model will both reduce the challenging behaviors that result from student frustration and increase the quality of student learning and performance. The philosophical foundation for this new classroom management approach is William Glasser's *Choice Theory* (1998). The classroom strategies that align with this foundation come from a variety of sources and educational experts: quality schools (Sullo, 1997), brain-based learning (Jensen, 1997; 1998), cooperative learning (Kagan, 1994), dimensions of learning (Marzano & Pickering, 1997), adventure-based learning (Rohnke, 1996), accelerated learning (Meier, 1999), and from my own 12 years as an English teacher.

In my experience leading in-service workshops, I've learned that teachers want practical, effective strategies that they can immediately implement in their classrooms. They do not want to be inundated with abstraction and rhetoric. Teachers don't have time. They have papers to grade, lessons to plan, parent contacts to make, and so on. Teachers do, however, want a clear rationale for any strategy before they will consider using it. This book provides both a rationale and literally hundreds of practical, effective teaching and managing strategies. Chapter 1 offers a concise explanation of Choice Theory, with an emphasis on the five basic needs that motivate all human beings, thus providing a rationale for the practical strategies explained throughout the rest of the book. Chapters 2 through 7 examine specific teaching and managing approaches that teachers can use to appeal to each of the five basic human needs in ways that improve the quality of student behavior and learning.

# Laying the Foundation for a Classroom of Choice

By definition, people are in a *teacher-student relationship* when two conditions are met: (1) the teacher has the knowledge and desire to impart information and skills to his students, and (2) the students are interested in learning the knowledge and skills that are being offered. These conditions are most consistently met with preschoolers and graduate students. Between those school years, the second condition is less consistently present. In order to increase the frequency of those teachable moments, management must occur.

## Teachers as Managers

Whether you are a teacher, a coach, or in any position in which you work with young people, you are first and foremost a manager. *Managing* is first creating the conditions for students to be interested in learning or performing, and then providing the structures, strategies, and activities that will encourage quality learning and quality performance. Teachers manage the learning space, time, materials, and the mental, physical, and emotional states of individuals, partners, small groups, and large groups. Effective teachers must be effective managers.

## Two Types of Motivation

One of a manager's most important concerns is the motivation of work-ers, or for our purposes, students. Unmotivated students do poor work or no work, learn very little, and often behave in irresponsible or disrup-tive ways. Motivated students do quality work, learn well, and behave responsibly. There are two approaches to motivating students. One appeals to *external motivation*, which relies heavily on incentives or rewards (positive reinforcement) and consequences or punishment (negative reinforcement). The other approach appeals to *internal moti-vation*, which depends on motivation to come from needs or drives within students.

### The Problems with External Motivation

External motivation is the most prevalent type of motivation used not only in classrooms, but also in the world at large. Think of the ways people try *to make* other people do what they want them to do. Whether it is a teacher trying to persuade a student to work, a parent trying to get a child to get ready for school, a wife trying to talk her spouse into doing a household chore, a boss trying to get his employees to work harder, or one nation trying to force another nation to change a policy or ideology, you will see one or more of the following strategies being used:

- *Asking:* Would you please do this?
- *Reasoning:* You should do this because . . .
- *Telling:* Just do it!
- *Rewarding (bribing):* If you do this, then you'll get that.
- *Appealing to the relationship:* Do it for me.
- *Negotiating:* If you do this, I'll do that.
- *Tricking:* I'll bet you can't do it in the next five minutes.
- *Reverse psychology:* Whatever you do, *don't do* it.
- *Shaming:* I'm so disappointed in you. I thought you could do better than that.
- *Nagging:* Have you done it yet? How about now? *Now?* Did you, huh, huh?
- *Yelling:* I said DO IT!
- *Threatening:* Do it or else . . .

- *Criticizing:* If you weren't so lazy, you'd do it.
- *Imposing consequences:* Because you didn't do it, you will lose this privilege.
- *Punishing:* Because you didn't choose to do it, you will have to . . .
- *Verbally attacking:* You are such a loser.
- *Humiliating:* Everyone, look at the blank expression on Leon's face.
- *Physically intimidating:* Invading personal space or pounding fist on table.
- *Physically forcing:* Shoving, spanking.

One of the problems with these strategies is that none is guaranteed to work. If a student or anyone else has the mindset to not comply, there is nothing you can do to make him, except possibly using physical force. Unless safety is the issue, that strategy is illegal in most schools. Besides, the behavior we are most interested in is learning, and you can't physically force anyone to learn.

Another problem with these external motivators is that they actually prevent learning from taking place. In *Teaching with the Brain in Mind*, Eric Jensen (1998) explains the effects of threats on the brain. Perceived threats, which could include many of the external motivation strategies previously listed from yelling to physical force create conditions that many students regard as highly stressful. When students are feeling highly stressed, "thinking and memory are affected . . . the brain's short-term memory and ability to form long-term memories are inhibited" (p. 53). Feeling highly stressed, students' brains tend to go into the fight-or-flight response, which may manifest in school through all kinds of acting out or withdrawing behavior. Clearly, "the stick" approach to motivation is counterproductive.

What then of "the carrot"? Surely rewards provide an incentive for students to behave appropriately and perform well? Actually, contrary to conventional wisdom, rewards are no more effective in motivating students than threats and punishment. In his book *Punished by Rewards*, Alfie Kohn (1993) examines the research on external incentives and concludes that the "do this and you'll get that" approach to motivation fails. Citing hundreds of studies, Kohn discusses the reasons that incentives such as stickers, pizza parties, free time, trips to the toy barrel, and even As do not work. The most important reason for teachers may be that "rewards change the way people feel about what they do" (p. 68). He explains that when a student hears "If you do this, then you'll get that," the message to the learner is "There must be something wrong with this if you have to give me that to get me to do it." Thus, what we are doing when we offer a reward for learning or following classroom rules, whether we realize it or not, is "killing off the interest in the very thing we are bribing them to do" (p. 72). Jensen echoes Kohn's concerns regarding rewards, warning that "students will want [rewards] each time the behavior is required; they'll want an increasingly valuable reward . . . [and that] the use of rewards actually damages intrinsic motivation" (1998, pp. 66–67).

Another problem with external motivators is that they tend to rupture relationships. Think of when you were last on the receiving end of any of the listed strategies, with the exception of asking. When we are feeling manipulated, either blatantly or subtly, the level of trust in the relationship is damaged. Subsequently, we are even less inclined to comply the next time that person tries to get us to do something. Therefore, the person trying to motivate us will most likely intensify the external motivation by either increasing the reward or moving down the strategy list from bribing to threatening or worse, further eroding the relationship.

## The Importance of Trustful Relationships in School

Back in the traditional "Don't-Smile-Until-Thanksgiving" days of classroom management, the relationship between students and teachers was simple. The belief was that it was not important if students liked or trusted their teachers as long as they respected or even feared them. More recently, the importance of the student-teacher relationship in developing an optimal learning environment has been better understood. For example, this relationship is an integral part of Dimension One of Robert Marzano's and Debra Pickering's *Dimensions of Learning* (1997) model and Alfie Kohn's *The Schools Our Children Deserve* (1999) approach to systemic school improvement. In their recent book *Trust in Schools*, authors Anthony Bryk and Barbara Schneider (2002) study the importance of social relationships to student learning and achievement. "Schools," state the authors, "are networks of sustained relationships. The social exchanges that occur and how participants infuse them with meaning are essential to a school's functioning" (p. xiv). In nationwide efforts to raise standards and improve student learning and achievement, trust is the key ingredient: "[A] broad base of trust across a school community lubricates much of a school's day-to-day functioning and is a critical resource as local leaders embark on ambitious improvement plans" (p. 5).

Although *Trust in Schools* examines the importance of trust at all levels in a school system (teacher-teacher, teacher-principal, school-parents, and so on), the authors emphasize the importance of strong teacher-student trust: "Trusting student-teacher relationships are essential for learning" (Bryk & Schneider, 2002, p. 31) The authors also say that a school can have abundant resources and effective teaching programs in place, but student learning will suffer if trusting relationships are not part of the formula. Furthermore, according to the authors, "Given [the] power asymmetry in the student-teacher role set, the growth of trust depends primarily on teachers' initiatives" (pp. 31–32). This responsibility is greatest at the primary level and gradually decreases as students mature and become more responsible for their own learning. This doesn't mean, however, that at the secondary level students are on their own and that trusting relationships in the classroom are no longer important. Older students simply have a little more responsibility for the classroom environment than they did as kindergartners or 1st graders. The teacher still makes the difference in the classroom.

Let us now examine the legacy of external motivating strategies listed previously in this chapter. Although coercive strategies, even "positive" ones such as rewarding, sometimes work for us in the short term, we must question the use of external control strategies considering the research on the importance of relationships in the classroom. I don't suggest that teachers immediately and unconditionally abandon the use of all external motivators. That could lead to chaos, especially in classrooms of students who have come up through a system that embraced external control. My recommendation is to gradually reduce external control and to do it with discussion about what you are doing and why. If students have learned to love stickers, for example, you might move from giving stickers to them for appropriate behavior or excellent work to having them award themselves stickers as they think they have earned them. With discussion, these students will begin to see that it is not the sticker, but their learning, that is important.

## Minimizing Fear and Coercion

In 1992, William Glasser—whose ideas provide the foundation for the practices and strategies explained in this book—published one of his best-known books, *The Quality School: Managing Students Without Coercion*. In the first chapter, Glasser explains that many of his ideas are school-based adaptations of the work of management guru W. Edwards Deming. Deming's place in management history is secured by his success in teaching a noncoercive management style to managers in the Japanese automobile and electronics industry after World War II (Glasser, 1992, p. 2–3). The result of Deming's work with the Japanese was dramatic. When Deming began working in Japan, the phrase "Made in Japan" was synonymous with cheap goods. Now, Japanese automobiles and electronics equipment are ubiquitous, and "Made in Japan" means high-quality products. Known as the American who taught the Japanese about quality, Deming is still well known in the Japanese industrial community; in his honor, the Japanese Union of Scientists and Engineers established the prestigious Deming Prizes for outstanding achievement in quality control (Aguayo, 1990). Glasser explains how Deming's ideas "can be brought into our schools so that the present . . . system, in which just a few students are involved in quality work, will be replaced by a system in which almost all students have this experience" (Glasser, 1992, p. 3).

The first condition necessary to encourage quality work and behavior, according to both Deming and Glasser, is to "eliminate fear and coercion." I respectfully modify that; instead of using the word *eliminate*, I prefer to say *minimize* fear and coercion. I make this modification for two reasons:

1. Schools are systems that have rules and consequences that teachers have no control over. For example, in many states, students are required by law to attend school until a certain age. Therefore, some coercion is built into the system.

2. Students may fear school or teachers because they previously had frightening experiences. Their current teacher may never threaten or coerce these students, but these students may feel a certain amount of trepidation around any teacher because of their personal history. Again, this is not something we can control.

Consequently, we cannot *eliminate* fear and coercion from our learning environments, but we can do our best to *minimize* them.

The essential question, then, is: How do we manage students' learning and behavior while minimizing coercion? Does that mean we adopt a laissez-faire, anything-goes teaching style? Not at all. The ideas in this book come from direct experience, not just from theory or clinical research. I know firsthand how students respond to a lack of structure, and it isn't pretty. What I am suggesting is that first we do all we can to appeal to what intrinsically motivates students. If that doesn't work, we can always return to the strategies we've used in the past. However, I am convinced that once you have experienced a class full of intrinsically motivated students, you will not want to go back. Choice Theory has worked for thousands of teachers throughout the world.

After a brief explanation of the model of intrinsic, or internal, motivation that is based on Choice Theory, the rest of this book offers concrete, proven strategies you can use to appeal to students' internal motivation.

## Choice Theory

Choice Theory, developed by William Glasser, is a psychological model that explains how and why human beings behave. According to Choice Theory, throughout our lives, the aim of all our behavior is to meet one or more of our innate basic human needs. One of the main tenets of Choice Theory, therefore, is that all behavior is purposeful. Now, observe a group of children in a relatively unstructured environment for a while and say to yourself, "All behavior is purposeful." The statement may seem ludicrous! Some of their behavior seems silly, some inappropriate, some antisocial, some even nonsensical, but the word *purposeful* doesn't come to mind. Some explanation is necessary. When I say all behavior is purposeful, I don't mean all behavior is effective or that all behavior is responsible. Choice Theory simply says that a purpose underlies all behavior. We are doing the best we can to meet our basic human needs given the knowledge, the skills, and the resources in our repertoire of behaviors. If we could think of a better way of achieving this purpose at any given time, we would choose it.

What are these basic needs that drive all of our behavior? There are five in all, one physiological need and four psychological. They are the need to survive, to love and belong, to gain power, to be free, and to have fun. Before you can effectively appeal to these needs in students, a clear understanding of each one is essential. In this chapter, I will provide a general explanation of each need. I would invite you, as you read about these needs, to think about their significance in your life. Later chapters will focus on the significance of each need in planning classroom activities and instruction.

## Survival

The physiological need to survive is often the first thing that comes to mind when we discuss basic needs. Survival includes the obvious needs for food, shelter, physical comfort, and safety. To meet this need, we sleep, wear clothing, seek shelter, and so on. However, because human beings have the ability to imagine the future, we do much more than attend to our immediate physical needs. We also think about our future security and physical health. We keep savings accounts, buy insurance, and invest in the stock market, bonds, and real estate. We exercise and diet with an eye on our waistlines. We plan for a comfortable retirement. Some of us invest in home security systems. So, the need to survive, though primarily physical, has a psychological component, our need for a sense of security in the future. In classrooms, students need to feel physically and emotionally safe and secure. Chapter 2 addresses specific ways teachers can help their students see the classroom as a safe, orderly learning community.

When we think of basic needs, physical needs may be the first that come to mind, but human beings require more than just physical well-being in order to lead happy, fulfilling lives. We have psychological needs as well. As you read about each of the following psychological needs, I invite you to think of the people, activities, things, and places in your life that help you satisfy these needs.

## Love and Belonging

Humans, like many other species, are social creatures. We live in family units, work on teams, form social and civic organizations, attend social gatherings, and engage in hundreds of other behaviors that help us connect and interrelate with others. Almost all human endeavors have some social dimension to them. Having a strong need for love and belonging is one of the reasons the human species has been so successful. In our primitive past, humans' urge to belong to a group manifested itself in cooperative hunting, gathering, child care, and defense of the group, behaviors that were essential to the other need we just discussed, survival. Therefore, though the need for love and belonging is primarily a psychological and emotional need, it is linked with the physical domain.

It is well known that newborns require a certain amount of physical affection in order to thrive. In his book *Love & Survival*, author and cardiologist Dean Ornish (1998), known for his success with the recovery of cardiac patients through changes in diet and exercise combined with meditation, concludes that there is a lifelong connection between the quality of our relationships and our physical and mental well-being. Citing hundreds of studies, Ornish says about the power of love and belonging: "I am not aware of any other factor in medicine—not diet, not smoking, not exercise, not stress, not genetics, not drugs, not surgery—that has a greater impact on the quality of life, incidence of illness, and premature death from all causes" (pp. 2–3). Studies such as those cited by Ornish support the Choice Theory principle that the deep-seated urge to love and belong—to connect with others, to cooperate, and to give and receive affection—is truly a basic need with a profound influence on our overall physical and mental wellness.

The need for love and belonging helps explain the importance of relationships in schools regarding student learning and achievement. Chapter 3 discusses the role this need plays in learning and describes more than 50 specific strategies that teachers can use to help them build those essential relationships with and among their students.

## Power

Power is the most frequently misunderstood need. For many people the word *power* is synonymous with dominance, authority, or control. For that reason, many do not want to admit they have an intrinsic need for power. When thoroughly understood in Choice Theory terms, the concept of power takes on a much broader, more positive meaning. People behave in three general ways when they attempt to meet their need for power:

1. *Power Over:* exercising one's influence over something or someone. This usage is the closest to the common perception of the word "power." A sculptor exercises power over her medium. The guitarist demonstrates power over his instrument. A mechanic exhibits power over an engine. These are examples of using power over inanimate objects, all positive. It is when people use or abuse power over other people that we see power in a negative light: The military junta hurried to exert its power over the nation; the chief executive officer enjoyed the benefits of money and power; the principal used his positional power to intimidate the staff. In each of these cases, someone is using power in an irresponsible way. Many use their influence with others for the greater good: Gandhi, Martin Luther King Jr., and Mother Theresa, to name a few. Power over is not, by definition, bad. Power over only becomes destructive if one is using power irresponsibly, depriving others of meeting their basic needs.

2. *Power Within:* obtained when developing the knowledge and skills that increase the quality of our lives. Gaining power within includes learning, achieving success, and enjoying the feeling of self-worth that comes with personal growth. Without the need for the power within, human beings would never have developed the culturally and technologically sophisticated world we live in today. Something innate in human beings drives us to set goals, to achieve them, to improve upon what others have done before us, and creatively adapt to new situations—the need for power within. Think of yourself and fill in the following blank: "I want to be good at _____." All the behaviors you fill in the blank are

ways that you use to meet your power need. For example, you might have listed teaching, parenting, being a friend, listening, coaching soccer, gardening, or playing piano. Helping students gain power is what school is really all about. I discuss this topic in greater depth in Chapters 4 and 5.

3. *Power With:* achieved when working cooperatively with others. It is the place where the need for power and the need for love and belonging intersect. If you think of the great achievements of the human race, they all resulted from humans working together or building on the achievements of those who came before them. The international space station is an example of what can result from achieving power with. It challenges the capacity of the mind to imagine the number of centuries and all the individual human beings it took to develop the technology, to plan, and to implement the building of a laboratory in space. The drive to achieve power with is something a classroom teacher can tap to help every student learn and achieve more. Chapters 4 and 5 provide insight into the need for power in a structured learning environment and lists dozens of ways that teachers can manage students so that both the students and the teacher can meet their power needs effectively and responsibly.

## Freedom

The need for freedom does not require much explanation. Throughout history, millions have died in the name of freedom. In the Declaration of Independence, Thomas Jefferson referred to freedom as one of humankind's "inalienable rights." We human beings need independence—autonomy—to control, as much as possible, the direction of our lives. The need for freedom can be divided into two major types:

1. *Freedom to:* involves having choices. Freedom to go where you want, say what you want, associate with whom you want, pursue an interest or a career, and so on. We are most aware of the need for freedom when we perceive it as being threatened. Think of a time when you were pressured into doing something or going somewhere you didn't particularly want to. A good deal of the frustration you feel in a

situation like that is your freedom to need tugging at you. Like all of us, students need to be able to make choices. In the interests of maintaining an orderly learning environment, providing choices does not mean students have license to do or say anything they want. In Chapter 6, we'll explore specific strategies that you can implement that provide students with dozens of ways of meeting their freedom to need in responsible ways.

2. *Freedom from:* refers to freedom from things that cause us physical or emotional discomfort, such as fear, stress, disrespect, or monotony. In classrooms, much of the freedom from need is provided for if there is a safe, structured environment developed using management strategies such as those described in Chapter 2. Because this need includes freedom from boredom and monotony, Chapter 6 describes how to integrate novelty and spontaneity into your classroom procedures and routines. Doing so will enliven the classroom for everyone and boost your students' interest in learning.

## Fun

I do not write about the need for fun last because it is the least important. Try to imagine life without enjoyment, laughter, or pleasure. Don't dwell on it; it is too depressing. People who find themselves in such circumstances often choose not to live any longer. Humans need to have fun, to play! The need for fun has particular significance to us as teachers. Glasser relates fun to learning: "Fun is the genetic reward for learning. We are descended from people who learned more or better than others. The learning gave these people a survival advantage, and the need for fun became built into our genes" (1998, p. 41).

As we play, we learn. Think of little children at play. What are they learning? They learn how to cooperate, negotiate, and get along with others. They learn how the world works: what dirt tastes like, how gravity works when you let go of a tree limb, how to use simple tools like a stick for digging to see where worms live. The old adage "Play is a child's work" is true. But play is not the domain of children only. Play is also the work of adults. Think of the creativity play inspires. Think of how play reduces stress. When was the last time you had a great, uncontrollable laugh? Didn't that feel wonderful? Didn't you feel relaxed afterward?

Play is essential for learning and for our physical and emotional well-being, but it also is a wonderful tool for building relationships. "It takes a lot of effort to get along well with each other, and the best way to begin to do so is to have some fun learning together. Laughing and learning are the foundation of all successful long-term relationships" (Glasser, 1998, p. 41). While many of the strategies in this book are fun, Chapter 7 specifies dozens of ways of rejuvenating the classroom with productive play.

## Important Characteristics of the Five Basic Human Needs

An understanding of the basic needs has the potential to transform a classroom. It is important to understand not only what the needs are, but also certain characteristics of the needs that have significant implications for classroom instruction and management. After an explanation of these characteristics, we will discuss their significance to the classroom.

First, the needs are *innate*. Another term for *basic human needs* would be *genetic instructions*. Just as other species have behavioral instructions as part of their genetic makeup, so do humans. Many species have specific genetic instructions: Canada geese are genetically instructed to migrate to the Chesapeake Bay; bears, to hibernate; and newly hatched sea turtles are instructed to dig out of the sand, get to the water, and start swimming. Other species are given genetic instructions also, but because of their more highly developed brains, the instructions are more general. The individual can use his intelligence to choose from a number of behaviors that will meet the instructions (or needs). Because of our well-developed cerebral cortex, humans' genes are not shouting instructions like "Fly south!" or "Go to sleep!" or "Swim!" Our genes are whispering things such as "Be physically comfortable and safe," "Connect with others," "Gain personal power," "Be free," and "Be playful!" We have free will in how we choose to behave or not behave in following these genetic instructions. One thing is not a choice, however. Just as it is not a choice for a Canada goose to feel the urge to fly south in November, it is not a choice for human beings to feel the urge to survive, love and belong, gain power, be free, or have fun. These needs are in our genes.

Second and third, the basic needs are *universal*, and people have the needs in *varying degrees*. In other words, though all human beings have all five needs, each of us does not experience the same amount of drive for each need. For example, one person might have a high need for love and belonging, with varying degrees for power, freedom, fun, and survival. That person's behavior would probably look different from the behavior of someone else who might have a high need for power and freedom, a moderate need for fun and survival, and a low need for love and belonging. The former might spend a great deal of time and energy on relationships, both in his personal life and at work. He (call him Dan) might attend social events, join clubs and civic associations, enjoy close relationships with friends and family, and enjoy his favorite activities most often in the company of others. The person with the higher need for power and freedom needs (call her Sheryl) might spend more time alone, working on projects, reading, attending courses, competing in athletics, constantly learning and achieving. Sheryl may have a few close friends but may not spend as much time with them as Dan spends with his. In Choice Theory terms, Dan and Sheryl have different *needs profiles*. A person's needs profile, the relative quantities of the five basic needs by which an individual is genetically motivated, does not dictate a person's behavior; but it is a powerful influence. The examples of Dan and Sheryl are not necessarily the way individuals with high love and belonging or power needs behave. They are simply ways these two individuals might manifest their particular needs profiles. Think about your own needs profile. If you were to list your needs in order from most important to least important according to their influence on your behavior, how would you order them?

Fourth, the basic needs often *conflict* with other people's needs. If, for example, a store manager has a high need for power and meets that need through frequently exerting what authority he has, he might easily come into conflict with an employee with a high freedom need. A classroom of students with a high need for fun and freedom might end up in trouble with a teacher who has a high survival need (order and security). I'd like to stress that in each of those cases, the individuals involved *might* come into conflict. It is not inevitable. People attempting to meet their different needs (or even the same need) in the same environment don't necessarily end up at odds. One of the main purposes of this book is to describe how to create the conditions in a classroom so that teachers and students can meet their needs effectively without coming into conflict.

## Responsible and Effective Behavior

Although all behavior has a purpose to meet one or more of our basic human needs, all behavior is not necessarily effective or responsible. The term *effective behavior* refers to a behavior that works for us; it satisfies our needs. The term *responsible behavior* refers to behavior that satisfies our needs without depriving others of meeting theirs. Unfortunately, not everyone chooses effective and responsible behaviors all the time. A student who calls out answers out of turn may be effectively meeting his power need but is depriving other students and the teacher of meeting theirs. The class clown may find that disrupting the class helps her meet her power, freedom, and fun needs; but again her behavior is depriving others (particularly the teacher) of meeting their needs effectively. The good news is that people can, and most are more than willing to, choose new, responsible behaviors if they are at least as needs-satisfying as their former, irresponsible behaviors. Chapters 2–7 discuss how to manage a classroom so that students are more likely to make responsible choices.

## Implications for the Classroom

This book explains only part of Choice Theory. However, an understanding of the basic human needs provides a solid foundation for creating and managing a high-quality learning environment.

An understanding of the five basic needs can help develop a rationale for management and instructional strategies that don't rely on time-consuming, ineffective extrinsic motivational practices. Students' genetic instructions are to seek a safe, orderly environment (survival), feel a sense of belonging, be successful and have a sense of importance (power), experience a sense of independence, and have fun. If we do not provide opportunities for students to meet these needs in our classrooms, the genetic instructions don't go away. Students will be frustrated. Some frustrated students will behave responsibly and just wait until they are home or at lunch to satisfy their unmet needs. Many others have not developed that much self-control and engage in irresponsible behaviors in their attempt to follow their genetic instructions. These irresponsible behaviors take on a million different faces. If you've been in any classroom, you've seen them, and I'm sure you'd agree that none of them add to the quality of the learning environment. These behaviors drive many teachers out of the profession and create the conditions for undue stress for the rest. Using effective teaching and managing strategies that provide students with opportunities to follow their genetic instructions responsibly prevents students from using disruptive behavior to meet their needs and turns the classroom into a joyful learning environment.

Just as each individual has a unique needs profile, so does each class, which may have an impact on the way you instruct and manage. One year when I was teaching high school English, I had a really difficult 11th grade class. The students in that class seemed to have no other purpose than to keep me from teaching them anything. And they were successful. A little more information about this class is necessary. It was a class of only 15. However, eight of the students were labeled "ED" (Emotional Disorders), and seven of them were labeled "LD" (Learning Disabled). These students had been experiencing difficulty with school since early elementary school; they knew they were labeled and, therefore, had low expectations of themselves. A couple of the boys wore their labels as a badge of honor. It was a challenging class, to say the least.

As I sat at my desk at home one weekend, pounding my head with my fist trying to figure out what to do with this class, I had a sudden insight. I had just taught a workshop to my school staff on Choice Theory, and the concept of the needs profile popped into my head. I thought about the behaviors I'd been observing in this class: refusing to work in pairs or groups, getting up out of their seats for inappropriate reasons, looking out the window, skipping class, doing no homework and little class work, and frequently taking the class off task by asking questions that didn't relate to the learning. All the disruptive, irresponsible behaviors I was thinking about pointed in one direction: the freedom need, both *freedom to* and *freedom from*.

So what? I thought. What would a class that is designed to meet the freedom need *and teach course content* look like? I had the rest of the weekend to ponder that question.

On Monday, I went into class, finally got their attention, and dramatically tossed my planning book in the garbage. I went on to tell them that what I'd been trying to do with them all year wasn't working. I had their attention; they were all listening to me at the same time! I told them that I wanted to help them become successful adults and that the communication skills I had to teach them were essential. So, in order for all of us to be successful, I told them, we were going to do things differently. Instead of my teaching the class as a large group, each individual student would be responsible for his own learning. I said I would provide the required assignments for each five-week increment. I would provide models, specific criteria, and any resources necessary for every assignment. I would be available for one-on-one instruction as they worked through the assignments. They could do the assignments in any order they chose. They could do them in class or take them home. But, in order to get credit for the course and to move on to 12th grade, these assignments must be completed.

I waited for the explosion, but instead got silence and sober expressions. One student asked what they could do if they finished the assignments before the end of the five weeks. I said they could either begin work on the next unit or bring in some appropriate reading material and read. The next question was the one I'd been waiting for: "So, Mr. Erwin, what do I gotta do to get outta here?" "Yeah," chimed in another student. It was music to my ears. We took the rest of the period to go through the syllabus until everyone had a clear understanding of the expectations. The next day, all of them showed up and all of them began their work, some more diligently than others. I can honestly say, though, that everyone did more work in that one period than they had all year up to that point. They didn't magically turn into eager learners, but the irresponsible behavior all but disappeared. Most important, all of the students improved as readers and writers that year, and all but one passed the class and went on to their senior year. Unfortunately, the one dropped out.

Sometimes the needs profile of a class can have profound implications for the best instructional and management strategies for that particular group of students. A class that has a high love and belonging need wants opportunities to work together, to share, to form and maintain relationships. One with a high power need may enjoy being listened to, being challenged, and gaining recognition for their successes. A group of students with high freedom needs, like the one above, craves choices, movement, and novelty. A class with a high fun need enjoys learning games, role-playing, and humor. One with a high survival need likes attention to safety, predictable procedures, and a sense of order. You can determine a class's needs profile the way I did, just by observation and making an educated guess, or you can teach the students about their needs and have them share with you an informal assessment of their own needs profile. Sometimes you may have a class that leans strongly toward one particular need, and you can adjust your managing and teaching accordingly.

More often, however, your classes will be composed of students with a wide assortment of needs profiles. Therefore, using a balance of needs-satisfying strategies will mean that everyone can get what they need at least part of the time. Remember that even in classes that lean strongly toward one need, the students in those classes have all five, so that you can't completely ignore them. Imagine a workplace where you enjoy strong relationships with your supervisor and colleagues, feel like you are a successful contributing member of the organization, enjoy a sense of autonomy, are encouraged to learn and play, and are provided with a salary that is sufficient and fair. Wouldn't that be a place where you'd be committed to doing quality work? It's the same for students. Providing students with a needs-satisfying learning environment not only prevents irresponsible behavior, it also encourages students to be engaged in quality learning by appealing to what intrinsically motivates human beings.

Another benefit of using needs-satisfying teaching and managing strategies is that they can simplify your planning. By using the strategies explained in this book, you will be simultaneously addressing a variety of learning styles, tapping into multiple intelligences, engaging both hemispheres of the brain, and practicing the teaching and managing strategies most strongly supported by educational research.

2

# Survival in the Classroom

WE MANIFEST THE PHYSIOLOGICAL NEED FOR SURVIVAL IN MANY OBVIOUS WAYS: BY eating, drinking, sleeping, wearing clothing, and seeking shelter, for example. However, as William Glasser (1998) states, we also manifest the need for survival in many subtle ways. The survival need not only entails basic physical requirements, it also involves our desire for a sense of order and security in our lives. Exercising, creating routines, investing, saving for retirement, and monitoring our fat intake are other ways that help us feel a sense of well-being. In school, most students are clothed and fed properly, but many experience threats, real or perceived, on a daily or hourly basis—threats from their peers, their teachers, and the school system.

From the time they line up at the bus stop to the time they get home in the afternoon, students are subject to physical and verbal threats from other students on the bus, in the halls, on the playground, and even in the classroom. I found that during my middle school lunch duty, for example, I spent a great deal of my time asking students to keep their hands to themselves and stop calling each other names. In many urban and some suburban schools, the existence of gangs creates a significant threat to students' safety. Well-publicized examples of school violence add to the anxiety many students feel during the school day.

Students also often perceive threats by teachers and other staff members. In many states, corporal punishment (the "board" of education) is still legal, and in many classrooms teachers attempt to achieve control through sarcasm, belittling, threatening, criticizing, and punishing. I've discovered that in students' minds being "yelled at" simply may consist of a whispered reminder of a rule or a glance in a student's direction. Although "He yelled at me!" may not be an accurate description of an event, it is truly the way many students perceive it. And as the saying goes, "Perception is reality."

Besides feeling threatened by other students and their teachers, children frequently feel threatened by the system itself. Poor or failing grades are the most common threat, but students also feel threatened by consequences such as being sent to the time-out room, going to the principal's office, having their name called over the public address system, being suspended, and being expelled. Further, all the activity that exists in any school populated by hundreds of students and dozens of teachers can make it seem chaotic. The seeming lack of order can itself be threatening.

Taken collectively, all of these perceived threats can have a devastating impact on learning. In *Teaching with the Brain in Mind*, brain research guru and educational consultant Eric Jensen (1998) tells us that stress reduces a student's ability to sort out what's important from what's not, impairs short- and long-term memory, and makes students more susceptible to illness. He goes on to say that chronic stress can trigger chemical imbalances in the brain, which can increase the chances that students will choose impulsive, even violent, behavior in their attempts to regain control over their lives.

Anything we can do to help students feel a sense of physical and emotional safety and security will improve their social behavior and help them perform better academically. This chapter will list and explain strategies teachers can use to help students meet their need for survival—not only their immediate physical needs, but also their need to have a general sense of safety, order, and security.

## Immediate Physical Needs

### Water

Not only do we need water for survival, but our brain also needs water to function properly (Jensen, 1998). Because the brain is about 78 percent water and we need water to maintain electrolytic balance, a trip or two to the drinking fountain for a couple of slurps a day is not enough. Students and teachers should drink at least eight, 8-ounce glasses of water each day. You might encourage students to bring water bottles to class or provide a drink pass that would allow students to go to the drinking fountain without disrupting class. A 3rd grade teacher I know has a fundraiser at the beginning of every year and uses the money to rent a water cooler for her room for the year. Of course, along with more water will come more trips to the restrooms. Again, a restroom pass or sign-out sheet would allow one or two students to leave the room without disruption. For my restroom pass, I used a small ceramic model of Grendel—the monster from the *Beowulf* legend—that a student made for me. A biology teacher in our school used a plastic model of a brain. Having students carry these somewhat peculiar objects to the bathroom helped me keep track of the number of students using the water fountain and bathroom and discouraged students from abusing the privileges as most students felt a little uncomfortable carrying a ceramic Grendel or plastic brain through the halls.

## Food

If you have your students all day or for a mid-morning or mid-afternoon class, you might encourage them to bring a snack. When a person's blood sugar is low, he tends to be tired, easily distracted, and irritable. Many teachers won't allow snacks because they fear the mess that might be created. Try it! In my experience, students appreciate the teacher's willingness to allow a snack so much that that they will rise to the occasion and be responsible for cleaning up.

Another idea is to have students take turns bringing snacks for everyone. My students really enjoyed this. They got into a kind of friendly competition, each student trying to outdo the others. I always made sure to provide a competitively yummy snack for students whose parents might object or who came from families who couldn't afford snacks for 25 to 30 students. You never saw kids clamber to get into a classroom like they did in that one. You can, of course, have guidelines regarding the kinds of snacks that are allowed in order to avoid the messy kind (anything gooey, poppy seed bagels, etc.) and the unhealthy kind (sugar-coated chocolate honey blasts).

## Oxygen

The brain uses one-fifth of the body's oxygen (Jensen, 1998). It is critical to learning to provide ways for students to get the oxygen-rich blood their brains need:

- *Open windows.* When possible, open windows to let some fresh air into the classroom.

- *Plants.* Our schools often have stuffy "institutional air"—air that has not been circulated properly. Get some houseplants into your classroom; they not only provide oxygen, they add a homey quality to the class environment. From my experience, spider plants and succulents require less water and are hardy.

- *Breathing and stretch breaks.* Once an hour or when you see their eyes glaze over, ask the students to stand up and lead them through a simple breathing exercise. Ask them to breathe in deeply, stretching their arms up as high as they can. Hold the breath for two counts and let the air out, lowering their arms. Make sure they expel all the "dead air" from their lungs. Repeat this three times and have them sit down. You'll be amazed at how much more alert, yet calm, the students will be.

- *Rag Doll.* Another breathing and stretching exercise is called Rag Doll. Have the students bend over from the waist and hang limply like a rag doll. Then direct them to slowly straighten up. As they straighten up, they are to take a deep breath and hold it for two counts. Next, exhale quickly and flop back into the rag doll position. Repeat the exercise two or three times.

- *Energizers.* Another way to get oxygen to your students' brains is to engage them in some of the energizer activities that are explained in Chapter 7. Energizers take very little time, but help students become reinvigorated and return to a productive learning state.

## The Need for a Sense of Safety, Security, and Order

### Greetings

Greet the students with a smile at the door as they come in. After the first day, greet them by name. This practice sends a message that you care about them and want them to feel comfortable in your room. It may take time away from your class preparations, but it is worth having students feel comfortable and safe in your classroom. You may want to customize your greeting with a "low five" or another special handshake to make it more fun for the students.

## Positive Posters

A great way to help reduce fear of failure and increase risk taking is to post positive messages about learning around the classroom. Messages such as "It's okay to make mistakes; that's how we learn" let students know that the classroom is a safe place and that they are not going to be punished for being human. In his book *Inspiring Discipline,* Merrill Harmin (1995) suggests using some of the following learning truths, to which I've added a few:

- We each learn in our own ways, by our own time clocks.
- It's intelligent to ask for help. No one need do it alone.
- We can do more and learn more when we're willing to risk.
- It's not mistakes that are important. It's what we do after we make a mistake.
- If it happened, it happened. Let's go on.
- Better is better.
- Everyone can learn and learn well.
- We are all intelligent, just in different ways.

Refer to these posted messages frequently, so that these truths about learning become part of the classroom culture, reassuring that your classroom is a risk-free learning place. Harmin recommends not using more than six or seven of these posters in any one classroom. Having too many signs might dilute their power.

## Guidelines for Behavior

Once you have established a code of conduct for the classroom, your job as the teacher is to make sure it is followed consistently. Whether or not you use the Classroom Constitution method I recommend in Chapter 4 to establish behavioral guidelines, rules such as keeping hands and feet to oneself and avoiding put-downs are sure to appear on the list. For a sense of safety to exist, the teacher must address any violation of these guidelines. Sometimes, in our haste to begin or complete a lesson, we'll allow a subtle putdown or a "harmless" poke to slide. That sends a message to students that the content is more important than maintaining a physically or emotionally safe place for everyone. I'm not recommending that the teacher overreact and severely punish the violator of the code of conduct, but unless the teacher addresses the behavior right then or immediately after class, the unwanted behavior will likely continue.

## Avoid Threatening, Bribing, and Punishing

Students watch every move teachers make, and they assume that the way the teacher treats one student is the way that same teacher will treat them. When teachers criticize, punish, or use sarcasm with any student in the class, the message is that this is not a safe place for anyone.

Bribes, frequently called "rewards" or "positive reinforcement," send a similar message. In his book *Punished by Rewards*, Alfie Kohn (1993) makes a powerful, well-documented argument about the use of incentives and rewards, stating that rewards have several drawbacks. One is that rewards can destroy students' interest in the behavior that is encouraged. Another is that the use of rewards can destroy relationships. Having examined literally hundreds of studies on the use of rewards, Kohn concludes the following:

> "Do this and you'll get that" turns out to be bad news whether our goal is to change behavior or to improve performance, whether we are dealing with children or adults, and regardless of whether the reward is a grade, a dollar, a gold star, a candy bar or any of the other bribes on which we routinely rely. Even assuming we have no ethical reservations about manipulating other people's behavior to get them to do what we want, the plain truth is that this strategy is likely to backfire. (1993, p. 47)

In *Teaching with the Brain in Mind*, Eric Jensen (1998) states: "From a social and educational context, rewards have . . . been studied and, to a large degree, rejected as a motivating strategy" (1998, p. 66). He explains that withholding a reward if a student does not meet the behavioral objective is perceived as a punishment and has the same impact.

The question, then, is how do we maintain order if we don't rely on the traditional methods of classroom control—positive and negative reinforcement? The purpose of this book is not to focus on discipline problems; it is to help teachers create a classroom environment where discipline problems do not become an issue. However, as Glasser (1998) states, even in a quality school there will be occasional discipline incidents, even if you have done everything you can think of to create a needs-satisfying environment and are teaching and managing effectively. Some alternatives to punishing and rewarding include:

- *Proximity.* Sometimes just walking within arm's length of a student will help the student readjust her behavior.

- *The general reminder.* Ask the students to evaluate themselves. Rather than call attention to any one student, simply ask, "Do you remember how important our class constitution is (or classroom rules are)? How well are we doing right now in following the class constitution we developed?" This often will help one student be aware of his behavior without disrupting the class.

- *What are you doing?* Sometimes students are not aware of their disruptive behavior. I remember when I was a middle school student and an avid rock drummer, I would sometimes irritate my teachers with my incessant finger tapping. It became such a habit that I was often unaware that I was even doing it. A teacher's asking me "What are you doing?" would have brought my behavior to my attention, and I would have stopped immediately.

- *The gentle reminder.* If you've developed a class constitution, calmly ask the student, "Do you remember what we agreed upon when we developed the class constitution? Would you please stop _____ or start _____ now? Thanks." If you have posted a list of rules, simply ask, "Would you please follow rule number __ right now? Thanks."

- *The teacher look.* You remember this one. In *The First Days of School*, Harry Wong and Rosemary Wong (1998) list the steps for an effective teacher look:

1. Stare at the student, not angrily, but stare. This step may be enough. You might be able to stop right here.
2. Move well into the student's personal space, bend down to her level and very quietly so that only she can hear, say her name.
3. Then tell her exactly what you want her to do or stop doing.
4. Then thank her, again saying her name.
5. Move out of her personal space. (p. 164)

This strategy, like all strategies, must be used with consideration for the student you are working with. Some students may behave aggressively when they think their personal space is violated. The teacher's facial expression, body language, and tone of voice are important here. The nonverbal messages should all say, "Because I care about you and respect you, I will not allow this behavior to continue." You might even say that to the student. Moving out of the student's space immediately after thanking her allows her to save face and avoids a power struggle.

- *Impose consequences.* Once you've tried some or all of the above strategies, you might discuss and impose consequences for unacceptable behavior. You don't need to apologize for imposing consequences; all systems and organizations have consequences for violation of rules. There are differences between consequences and punishments, however. Examples of these differences are shown in Figure 2.1. Certain student behaviors often result in punishment. Figure 2.2 offers examples of possible alternatives to typical punishments for student behaviors.

- *Individual counseling.* If a student repeatedly behaves in ways that disrupt the learning environment or that put his own academic success at risk, individual counseling may be necessary. In these circumstances, teachers often send students to the school disciplinarian or school counselor for "correction." My experience is that counseling is much more effective if it is done by the teacher with whom the student is experiencing difficulty. One-on-one counseling also can have the benefit of significantly improving the relationship between that student and teacher. The trust and mutual respect that develop during teacher–student counseling

## FIGURE 2.1

### Differences between consequences and punishments

| Consequences | Punishments |
|---|---|
| Are known ahead of time | Are imposed after the fact |
| Are fair and reasonable | Are excessive |
| Are best when they are natural or at least relate to the offense | Are usually unrelated to the offense |
| May be developed with the help of the students | Are imposed by the teacher |
| Are imposed without emotion | Are imposed with anger |
| **Result in conformity to the rule** | **Result in resentment, rebellion, and resistance** |

## FIGURE 2.2

### Possible alternatives to punishments for student behavior

| Behavior | Punishment | Consequence |
|---|---|---|
| A student comes in late. | The student is sent to the office. | The student misses the learning that took place and must get notes from another student or the teacher on his own time. |
| A student continually interrupts during a class meeting. | The student must come to the classroom at lunch time and write, "I will not interrupt class meetings" one hundred times. | The student is asked to sit outside the class meeting circle until she is willing to follow the class meeting ground rules, at which time she returns to the circle. |
| A student does not bring a pen or pencil to class. | The student is sent to the assistant principal with a referral for being insubordinate. | The student borrows a pen from the teacher and leaves a shoe or another appropriate item as collateral until he returns the pen. |

encourage greater cooperation and increase the likelihood that the student will choose more responsible behavior.

A counseling process aligned with the ideas expressed in this book is William Glasser's *reality therapy*. Although reality therapy is too involved to discuss in detail here, you can quickly and easily learn a few simple questions that can help a student make more effective, more responsible choices. In brief, reality therapy is a questioning technique that helps people

1. Identify specifically what they want in the present situation;
2. Examine what they are currently doing;
3. Evaluate the effectiveness of their current behavior; and
4. Develop a plan that has a better chance of succeeding, assuming that what they are doing is *not* working to the extent that they would like it to (Glasser, 1992, pp. 142–145).

Learning these five questions can help you guide students to make better choices:

1. What do you want in regard to _____ (the class, their relationship with their peers, etc.)?
2. What are you currently doing regarding _____?
3. Is what you are doing getting you what you want?
4. Are you willing to try something different?
5. What is something that might work better for you?
   (Glasser, 1992, pp. 142–145)

For a more detailed explanation of the process of reality therapy, read William Glasser's *Counseling with Choice Theory* (2000a), Robert Sullo's *Inspiring Quality in Your School* (1997), or Robert Wubbolding's *Using Reality Theory* (1988).

## Procedures and Routines

According to recent brain research, an ideal learning environment provides "a rich balance of novelty and ritual" (Jensen, 1998, p. 50).

Novelty grabs students' attention and helps get them to an optimal learning state. Chapter 6 will address strategies that provide novelty. What Jensen refers to as "rituals," I call "procedures" and "routines." A *procedure* is simply the way something is done in a classroom. A *routine* is a procedure that has been used enough that it becomes automatic. Using effective procedures and routines provides students with structure—the sense of order and security that students' genetic instructions for survival demand.

Education experts Harry Wong and Rosemary Wong (1998) make an important point when they state that "the number one problem in the classroom is not discipline; it is the lack of procedures and routines" (p. 167). In classrooms I've visited where procedures were either poorly thought out or lacking, there was a great deal of confusion and time off task, often resulting in unproductive classes and inappropriate student behavior. Developing effective procedures can make the difference between an orderly, efficient classroom and chaos. The following classroom situations require procedures:

- Entering the classroom and settling down to work
- Taking roll
- Quieting a class
- Getting the teacher's attention
- Collecting written work
- Moving from place to place
- Sharpening a pencil
- Practicing safety drills
- Asking a question
- Entering the class when tardy or after an absence
- Working with a substitute teacher
- Holding class meetings
- Leaving the classroom when dismissed
- Exchanging papers
- Giving directions so that you don't have to repeat yourself

I'm sure you can think of other situations specific to your classroom where you might need routines.

I'm not recommending that you develop such a rigid classroom that it feels like boot camp. Too many procedures can take all the freedom and spontaneity out of a classroom. However, procedures are a part of the real world. Society has generally recognized procedures for answering a telephone, greeting each other, purchasing movie or concert tickets, voting, and so on. Procedures help make the world and the classroom run more smoothly, imparting a sense of order.

In the following pages, I've explained some procedures for circumstances that most teachers encounter in the classroom. These are procedures that have either worked well for me or for other teachers I know. It isn't important that you use these specific procedures. The important thing is that you develop effective and efficient procedures that work for you and your students. I also recommend reading books that focus on procedures exclusively, such as Harry Wong's and Rosemary Wong's *The First Days of School* (1998), to gather some helpful ideas for many other classroom procedures.

### Entering the Classroom and Settling Down to Work

**Journal Writing or Sponge Activity.** Students come into the classroom, move quickly to their desks, take their learning journals out of their desk or pick them up from a designated shelf or bin, find their journal assignment for that day, and begin to write or work. It's a good idea to keep the journals in the room, so students don't disrupt the procedure by saying, "I forgot my journal." Having the assignment in the same place on the board or on a flip chart, or on the overhead prevents any confusion over where students should look for it.

This strategy can work in any class. In math or science, pose a problem related to the previous day's learning or to the learning coming up that day. In social studies, ask a question about the events studied the previous day or in the reading. In English, students can brainstorm a writing assignment, react to literature, or begin free writing a story that may be later turned into a final draft. In art, students can discuss the progress they're making on their current project. In any class, students can ask questions about the content, engage in a dialogue with the teacher, or begin a response to a question that will springboard a class discussion.

This procedure, sometimes called a *sponge* because it soaks up often wasted time, allows the teacher time to take roll or take care of some of the other tasks she had to give up in order to greet the students at the door. Getting the students immediately engaged creates an orderly atmosphere and increases time on task.

## Quieting a Class

**Signal and Response.** A tried-and-true quiet signal is simply to raise your hand and have the students raise theirs, too, so that students who may not be looking at you will see other students with their hands raised. Another method that works particularly well for younger children is to clap your hands three times and have them clap three times in response.

**Wind Chimes.** A pleasant sound like wind chimes or a call bell works well with any age. This works better than a visual signal when children are working in cooperative groups because often half the children in the class have their backs to the teacher and can't see a visual cue. Teach students that when they hear the chimes or bell, they are to finish their conversations within five seconds and turn their attention to you. Wind chimes can be purchased at any department store, and most office supply stores carry call bells.

**Lights Out.** Simply switch the lights off and on and count backwards from five. When you get to zero, all students should be silent, and all eyes on you.

**Sound Effects.** For a little humor, use a sound effects tape. Tell students, "When you hear the breaking glass, finish your thoughts and focus your attention on me." You can purchase sound effects tapes at most chain music stores or from drama supply stores or catalogs. Often you can match the sound effect you use to the season: evil laughs in October, sleigh bells in winter, and so forth.

**Consistent Verbal Message.** Instead of "Okay, everybody, quiet down," I like to use, "Please pause and focus on me." Using a consistent verbal message that all students understand avoids misinterpretation. To ensure the effectiveness of a verbal message, you might combine it with one of the other strategies explained previously.

## Students Seeking Help

"Do you want your students to raise their hands when they want help, wigwagging their arms to attract your attention, calling your name at the same time, stopping work in the process accompanied by muttering and complaining to their classmates because you do not respond instantly?" (Wong & Wong, 1998). Assuming the answer is "no," there are some alternatives.

**Hand Signals.** Students raise a predetermined number of fingers to signal to the teacher their request:

- One finger (the index finger, preferably): "I want to sharpen my pencil."
- Two fingers: "I need your help."
- Three fingers: "I'd like to go to the drinking fountain."

**Red Light, Green Light.** Make four-inch diameter circles out of red and green construction paper, glue them together, and if possible laminate them. Give one of these "desk dots" to each student. When they are working either independently or in cooperative pairs or groups, instruct them to put the desk dots on their desk *red side up if they need your assistance* and *green side up if they are doing well on their own.*

A variation of desk dots that works well for older students is a bookmark that is red on one side and green on the other. Use the same procedure as before when they are working independently or cooperatively. Older students will be less resistant to using bookmarks than something they may perceive as too childish, such as desk dots.

**Index Card.** Take a 6" x 8" index card and fold it into a three-sided pyramid. On one side, write "Help, please." On the other, write "Please keep working." Place the card on the student's desk so that the blank side is facing the child. When the student wants help, he places the card on his desk so that "Help, please" side faces the teacher. At the same time, the card reminds him to "Please *keep working.*"

**Textbook.** Another simple procedure is to use the textbook as a signal. When the student wants help, she stands her textbook up on her desk and *continues to work.*

## Collecting Student Work

**Crates.** You can buy plastic crates cheaply at most department stores or office supply stores. Students deposit their written work neatly in the crate on their way in or out of the classroom, depending on whether you are collecting homework or class work. Use different color crates for different classes or different subjects.

**Across the Rows.** Most of us have learned through our own school experience that the way to collect papers is to have students pass them down their row. We simply continue to use the procedure we grew up with. In *The First Days of School*, Wong and Wong (1998) list the problems with this age-old procedure:

1. If papers are passed up the row, you cannot see what is happening behind each student's back as you stand in the front waiting for the papers. Passing papers across the rows allows the teacher to stand at the side of the class and monitor the procedure.

2. Some students whack or poke the student in front of them to announce that the papers are coming down the row. This just creates an opportunity for further classroom disturbance.

3. There are frequently more students up a row than across a row. Thus passing the papers across the rows is more efficient.

The procedure itself is simple. Have the students at one side of the room place their papers on the desks of the student next to them. Then those students place their paper on top and repeat the procedure. If you have the students place the papers on the desks rather than in the hands, you avoid dropped papers. You can then collect the papers or have a student collect them at the end of each row. If students are sitting in groups or at tables instead of rows, designate a spot for the students to place their papers. Then you or a designated student collects them.

## Teach Procedures

If we want our procedures to work, explaining them is not enough; we need to teach them. To teach them properly, Wong and Wong (1998) recommend three steps:

1. *Explain:* Tell the students how to accomplish each procedure. Writing down and posting the steps would be helpful.

2. *Practice:* The first time you want to use the procedure, take the students through it until they all understand and can follow it the way you want it to be.

3. *Support:* Each time you use the procedure, remind students of what you expect, and repeat with those who do not follow the procedure properly. Avoid showing anger or criticizing students. Calmly ask the individuals who need the practice to repeat the procedure. Eventually, the procedure will become a routine.

## Anger Management

Students in classrooms where anger management is taught, modeled, and practiced feel safer, and students who have developed successful anger management skills feel a sense of self-control. Sometimes students come into the classroom angry about something that happened at home, on the way to school, or in the hallways. On other occasions, students become angry over something that happens in the classroom. There are a few ways you can help students manage their anger safely and effectively.

### The Behavioral Car

Teaching students Choice Theory concepts has many positive results, one of which is successful anger management. First, students need to understand the concept of *total behavior* (Glasser, 1998). Total behavior is more than just what people are doing. Along with their actions, it includes their thoughts, feelings, and physiology. All four of these components are present all the time. We are often more aware of one component than others, but every behavior includes all four. For example, if I am running, the most obvious component is the acting component. However, while I am running, I may be thinking, "What a beautiful spring morning!" Along with that action and thought, I may feel a sense of well-being and exhilaration. The physiological component would include elevated heart and breathing rates, sweating, and endorphin production. All four components would be the total behavior of running. When one component changes, they all change. If, for example, my thought changes from "What a beautiful spring morning!" to "Oh, no, here comes that bad-tempered pit bull," my actions, feelings, and physiology will change accordingly. My 8-minute-per-mile pace may change to a sprint, my feelings may change from well-being to fear, and my adrenal gland may go into high gear.

Once students understand that behavior is made up of four components—acting, thinking, feeling, and physiology—you can introduce Glasser's analogy of the behavioral car. The four components of total behavior can be seen as the four wheels of a car. When one wheel moves, the other three move simultaneously. We have the most control over our acting and thinking. Those are the front wheels, which we directly control with the steering wheel. Feelings and physiology are the back wheels, which follow along. Thus, anger—a feeling—is one of the back wheels.

Letting our anger drive our thinking, acting, and physiology is like trying to drive a car from the back seat. Students will understand immediately how senseless that is. Putting the concept of total behavior in concrete terms by using the car analogy helps all students understand the concept. It also allows you to help them to evaluate their own behavior by asking them questions based on the analogy. If a student begins to act out of anger, you can ask him, "Are you driving from the back seat or the front seat?" If a student says something like, "Johnny made me mad," you might respond, "Are you letting Johnny drive your car? or "Did you give Johnny your car keys?" You can also ask the following questions:

- Is your car on the road or in the ditch?
- Who is driving your car?
- Who has the keys to your behavioral car?
- Where is your car going to end up if you keep driving it this way?
- Are you steering your car where you want to go?
- Are you looking where you are driving?

Some teachers give each student a set of car keys at the beginning of the year, telling them, "These are the keys to your behavioral car. No one can take them away from you unless you give them away." If you use the car analogy with your students, I'm sure you and your students will find other ways of relating the analogy to specific situations.

## The Behavioral Traffic Circle

Expanding on the car analogy, I developed an activity I call the Behavioral Traffic Circle. You begin this activity by dividing the class up into pairs or small groups, giving each a toy car and a big sheet of chart paper or newsprint. Have the students draw a traffic circle with four exits. To save time, you might want to provide them with the traffic circles. If you laminate several traffic circles, you can use them year after year. Just have the students write on them with transparency pens. Next, you give each group of students a scenario that they might respond to with anger. One scenario might be the statement: "Brittany just called you stupid." The pairs or groups then generate three or four different possible choices of total behavior, one for each exit on the traffic circle. Next to each exit the students identify the acting, thinking, feeling, and physiology involved in each choice. For example, one behavior that a student might choose to respond to Brittany would be to call her a name. Next to one exit, the students would write the following:

DOING: Calling Brittany a jerk.

THINKING: "I hate her. She is so mean."

FEELING: Angry.

PHYSIOLOGY: Hot, sweating, tense, heart beating fast.

Another exit might offer the following responses:

DOING: Focusing on schoolwork, ignoring Brittany.

THINKING: "I'm not going to let Brittany drive my car."

FEELING: Calm.

PHYSIOLOGY: Cool, relaxed.

After the students generate three or four choices, ask them to identify the destination to which each total behavior might take them. The first choice about Brittany might result in the teacher doling out consequences, so the students might name that destination "Trouble Town." The second choice may result in the student feeling proud of himself for his self-control. Maybe the students would call this "Prideburg."

Finally, ask the students to drive their car down the exit that has the best chance of taking them where they want to go. This activity teaches students in concrete terms that in any given situation, choices always exist. Even if we are angry, what we *do* and where we drive our car is up to us.

## The Deep Breath and Positive Thought

As a child and adolescent, whenever I would become angry or upset, my mother would say, "Take a deep breath." Decades later, it's become common knowledge that deep breathing does indeed help us calm ourselves emotionally and physiologically. Combining this deep breathing with a pleasant thought is even more effective.

When my son Nathan was about 4 years old, my wife Nancy and I began teaching him this strategy. We waited for an opportune moment. One afternoon when all was well and he was in good spirits, we asked him to find the most comfortable place in the house to sit. He decided on an overstuffed chair in the living room. We then had him sit there and directed him to take several slow, deep breaths. Next, I asked him how he felt, and he said he felt good. After that, we asked him to think of a happy thought. He decided on "Mommy and Daddy love me." We then asked him if he would be willing to try this the next time he started to feel angry or upset, so he could calm himself down and not end up in his bedroom for a "time-out." He agreed.

We didn't have to wait too long. A day or so went by, and he didn't get his way about something. He started to work himself up into a minitantrum; his back wheels started to rev up, so to speak. We guided him to the comfortable chair he had chosen and reminded him to take slow, deep breaths. Then we had him think his happy thought to himself. In moments, he was calm and ready to quietly work out his issue.

After a period of this kind of guided practice, he was able to calm himself down without our help. For a while we needed to say, "Nathan, calm yourself down," but eventually he would simply go sit down and take himself through the process.

In 1st grade, his teacher called home one day to tell us about an incident in which a boy threw a rock at Nathan on the playground. She said, "It was amazing. Instead of throwing a rock back at the boy, he went over to the curb, sat down, started breathing and saying something to himself. He calmed himself down in seconds." This practice has served him well. He now holds an advanced belt in karate and could, if he were not able to control his temper, seriously hurt someone. Combined with the discipline he learns in his martial arts training, this technique helps him make positive choices even when he's angry.

Having your students identify a positive thought and practice deep breathing when they are calm might be something that would help them compose themselves when their back wheels are revved up. Like Nathan, students will need some guided practice at first, but once they learn this anger management technique, it will serve them well the rest of their lives.

### The Comfortable Chair

To deal with angry or frustrated students in the classroom, you might provide a comfortable chair if students need to give themselves some time out. If, for example, a student becomes angry when he receives an incomplete on an important assignment, he could choose or be invited to sit in the comfortable chair until he can calm himself down and return to class, or until you have a chance to conference with him. If this student has already learned deep-breathing and positive-thinking skills, he should be encouraged to use that skill in the comfortable chair. You can buy a comfortable chair reasonably at a used furniture store or the Salvation Army Thrift Shop. Or consider using a beanbag chair, which can be purchased new for a reasonable price.

## Other Strategies That Create a Safe, Orderly Classroom Environment

### Daily or Weekly Agenda

How many times a week do you hear, "What are we doing today?" Posting a written agenda of the class or the day will eliminate that question, help students see that there is an organized plan, and reduce their fear of the unknown. Simply write, or have a student write, a brief agenda of the class or day on the chalkboard, a flip chart, or on the overhead, and place it in the same place every day.

## Team-Building Activities

Many of the team-building activities explained in Chapter 3 will help students trust you and their peers by helping them feel safe and secure. In addition to the activities explained in that chapter, many books are available on the topic of team building, including Mary Henton's *Adventure in the Classroom*, Karl Rohnke's *Silver Bullets,* Sandy Stewart Christian and Nancy Loving Tubesing's *Instant Icebreakers*, and Spencer Kagan's *Silly Sports and Goofy Games*.

## Journal Communication

Many students feel more comfortable communicating their thoughts and feelings in writing than they do face-to-face with their teacher. If journal writing is part of your daily procedures, it can be an excellent opportunity for students to communicate to you any fears or concerns they are experiencing in the classroom. You must let them know that what they write in their journal is confidential, unless what they communicate is something that you are mandated by law to report to outside agencies. Explaining your confidentiality policy helps build trust and encourages them to confide in you. It is also important that you respond to their writing in a timely manner. It is almost impossible to read each student's entire journal, especially if you are using journals on a daily basis. One way you can make sure you read the important journal entries and protect yourself from litigation is to ask the students on a weekly basis to place an asterisk next to the journal entries that they really want you to read. Make sure you read and respond to those and any others you have time for.

## Music

William Shakespeare tells us, "Music oft hath such a charm to make bad good" (*Measure for Measure*, IV, *i*, 16). Why not put such a charm to use in the classroom? Certain kinds of music help create an atmosphere of calm and order. Baroque music, almost anything by Mozart, and the music of many New Age musicians such as George Winston work well. Avoid pop music, rock, dance, or other high-energy forms of music if what you want is to develop a sense of order. Some of the best times to play soothing music are

- When the students are entering the room,
- When students are writing in their journals,
- When you are engaging the class in breathing or stretching breaks, and
- When students are working quietly at their desks.

### Manners

Many students do not learn manners at home. Teaching students basic social skills sends the message, "In this classroom, we treat each other with courtesy." When a classroom is a courteous environment, students feel safer and many discipline problems are avoided.

Chapter 3 has an extensive section on teaching manners to help students feel a sense of connectedness. Some of the simple manners to teach students are

- Greeting each other with a handshake instead of a punch,
- Saying please and thank you,
- Saying "Excuse me" if a student steps in front of someone,
- Apologizing when it is appropriate,
- Covering a cough or a sneeze, and
- Waiting until someone is finished speaking before making a comment or asking a question.

Manners can be taught formally through manners lessons or informally through modeling, gentle reminding, or talking to students one-on-one. The age of the students and the nature of the class you teach will determine how manners are integrated into your classroom.

## Conclusions

We often take the satisfaction of students' physical needs for food, water, and oxygen for granted. Most schools have some kind of breakfast and lunch program, water fountains are usually available, and we assume they are breathing. But, by making sure we optimize students' blood sugar, water, and oxygen levels, we can help improve the quality of their learning. Furthermore, by creating physically and emotionally safe, orderly environments, we can reduce the stress that can inhibit our students' abilities to concentrate and perform. Paying attention to the students' need for survival also sends the message that you care about them, further enhancing your relationship. We will see in Chapter 3 that this enhanced relationship has important benefits.

# 3

# Love and Belonging
# in the Classroom

*The way is long—let us go together.*
*The way is difficult—let us help each other.*
*The way is joyful—let us share it.*
*The way is ours alone—let us go in love.*
*The way grows before us—let us begin.*
                    —Zen Invocation (Harris, 2000, p. 103)

IF YOU THINK ABOUT WHAT YOU MOST ENJOYED ABOUT GOING TO SCHOOL, THE first thought that pops into mind is probably not solving equations in Ms. Jones's 3rd-period algebra class or drafting your English essays in Mr. Smith's 7th-period study hall. Most likely what comes to mind is being with your friends; connecting with a special teacher whom you liked and respected; performing as a member of a sports team, musical group, or the cast of a play. Whatever it was, it probably involved at least one of the more important relationships in your life at the time. As we learned in Chapter 1, the intrinsic need to love and belong drives us to form connections in all the contexts of our lives: at home, at work, or at play.

Imagine yourself entering a new classroom in a new school for the first time. You don't know anyone; you feel completely alone. What is your first goal? Is it to learn something new in math, science, English, or social studies? No, it is to connect with someone, to feel like you belong.

Once you've made that first satisfying connection—with another student, a cooperative learning team, or with the teacher—you are ready to participate as a productive member of the class. Now you are ready to learn. Some teachers let this kind of connection happen by chance. Effective teachers create connections by design.

According to brain research, all effective learning has a social component. To help prepare for an optimal learning experience, teachers can create a sense of connection from the start. "Get students out of isolation and into community and you will help their learning immeasurably" (Meier, 1999, p. 33). As Robert Marzano states, "Students who feel accepted usually feel better about themselves and school, work harder, and learn better. Your job as a teacher begins with helping students to feel accepted by both you and their peers" (1997, p. 16).

## Connecting with Your Students

As I described in my introduction, I broke the old-school rule, "Don't smile until Thanksgiving," the day after Labor Day when my first class of 7th graders arrived. When I realized what I had done, I held my breath and waited for the inevitable. However, instead of taking over, tying me to my chair, and starting a wave of destruction, my students smiled back. As it turned out, it was the beginning of a wonderful year.

Although it is important to let students know that you hold high expectations for classroom behavior, their first impression of you does not have to be that of a 19th century headmaster. As Glasser states in *The Quality School*, "The better students know the teacher, and the more they like what they know, the harder they will work for him or her" (1992, p. 48). Intentionally developing relationships takes time, and many teachers might balk at using classroom time in ways that do not directly address the school or state curriculum. In my experience, as well as that of many other teachers, developing positive and healthy relationships with students not only encourages academic success, it also prevents discipline incidents. It is an investment that pays off in the long run. Teachers can efficiently and effectively foster positive relationships with their students in many ways.

## The Name Factor

To most of us, our name is precious; it's an important part of who we are. When someone uses our name appropriately, it feels good. We gain a sense of importance and recognition. When someone mispronounces, misspells, or forgets our name, it suggests that we aren't significant enough to get it right. Learning and using our students' names comprise the first step toward developing a positive relationship. Some teachers are in a position to learn students' names even before the students are assigned to them. As Robert Sullo explains, "many of the teachers in my children's school have taken the time to learn all the children's names. The teachers greet them [by name] regardless of the classroom they are in. The dividends that effort pays are enormous" (1999, p. 95). Not all of us are in a situation to do this: a 9th-grade teacher in a high school, for example. What we all can do, though, is familiarize ourselves with the names on our class roster as soon as possible. Then, on the first day of class, we can ask our students what they prefer to be called. For students with names that are difficult to pronounce, we can ask them to pronounce their name first before we unintentionally mangle it. Some ways to help us and the students in the class remember names include the following:

- *Nametags with symbols.* Have students create a nametag with the name they prefer to be called and a symbol that says something about them. For example, I might make a nametag that says, "Mr. Erwin" and draw a picture of a drum on it. When my class shared our names and symbols, I'd explain that one of my hobbies is playing the drums. This helped us learn everyone's name and a little personal information about each other.
- *Name cards.* Give the students 8 ½" x 11" pieces of poster paper and ask them to fold the paper in half lengthwise so that it can stand up. On one side ask them to write the name they prefer to be called. They might include a symbol, as explained previously, or you might have them decorate the name cards with markers or glitter pens so that each is unique. Then they can stand their name card on their desks with their name facing you. If they change classes, they can put their name cards in the textbook for your class and use them for a few days until they are no longer needed.

- *Names with adjectives.* This is a game that helps everyone in the class learn everyone else's name and helps develop listening skills at the same time. First, have the class sit in a big circle. Next, ask each student to come up with an adjective that might describe him or her that begins with the same sound as his or her first name: Jolly Jim, Caring Colleen, Zany Zachary, etc. Ask one student to begin by stating his name with the adjective. The student to his left repeats his name and then adds hers. The next student repeats the first two names and adjectives and adds his. As you go on, the students face a greater and greater challenge. Remind them that this is not meant to be stressful; it's just for fun and to learn each other's names. It's okay to make a mistake, and it's okay to help someone out. You'll be surprised at how quickly you will learn 25 new names.

 *Caution:* When the students are choosing their adjectives, ask them to choose positive words; sometimes the adjectives stick.

- *Bumpety-bump-bump.* This is another game that can help everyone in the class learn everyone else's name. First, have everyone stand in a circle while you stand in the middle. Explain that you'll start out in the middle, but that many others will have that opportunity soon. The person in the middle spins around pointing her finger at the students. (Explain that in this game it is not impolite to point.) Suddenly the person in the middle stops, points at one student, says his name followed by "bumpety-bump-bump" (e.g., "Tamara bumpety-bump-bump").

    Now that student must say the first names of the students on both her right and her left before the person in the middle finishes saying "bumpety-bump-bump." If Tamara is successful, the person in the middle repeats what she just did, choosing a different student. If Tamara is unsuccessful, she goes in the middle and the person who was in the middle joins the circle. And the game goes on.

- *Connect-a-name.* This activity creates a great visual that will also help classmates understand the concept of interdependence. Start out by asking one student who has a comparatively long name, like Jennifer (not Sue), to print her name on the chalk-board, whiteboard, or flip chart. Then ask someone to volunteer to be next, using one of the letters in Jennifer's name as one of the letters in his name. Soon you'll have what looks like a carefully constructed crossword puzzle (see Figure 3.1). When completed, leave the names exhibited for a while so that students can enjoy seeing their names interconnected as members of a team, and so that they can refer to the puzzle to remember each other's names (Rohnke, 1996).

### Pre-First Day of School Letter

Another way you can begin connecting with students before they enter your classroom is to send them a letter during the summer. If your class roster is completed before the middle of August and the numbers of students in your schedule allow, you might send them a letter that would

- Introduce you (your name and the subject or grade level you teach);
- Tell them that you are looking forward to having them in your class;
- Briefly explain one interesting or fun activity they will experience this year; and
- Tell them your room number and give directions, if necessary.

You might include a little personal information ("I hope you have a chance to do something fun and exciting this summer. My family and I spent a week backpacking in Maine."). This gives you the opportunity to tell your students what they will need, to be prepared for your class on the first day of school. Kids love to receive mail, and if the letter is upbeat, it will help your students develop a positive perception of you before they walk in the door.

### Greet Students at the Door

One simple way of making sure you connect in a positive way with all of your students every day is to greet them on their way in the room.

---

FIGURE 3.1

Example of Name Puzzle for Connect-a-Name

---

```
        JONATHAN      MARIE
        E   N    A      A
        N   N   TREVOR
        NED      E   E  KIRSTEN
        I            R
        FURAHA        ABRAHAM
        E
        R
```

---

Smiling and saying good morning to each student by name helps create a positive tone. It also affords you the opportunity to informally diagnose each student's emotional state and prevent behavioral problems that might happen in your classroom because a student has brought some emotional "baggage" from home or a previous class. Some teachers like to include a handshake or high-five with the greeting. Also, the more teachers who are visible in hallways when students are passing from class to class, the fewer the discipline incidents in the halls.

## The First-Day Test

Students come into every classroom with a head full of perceptions. Unfortunately, too often their perceptions of "teacher" are negative. The title "English teacher" or "math teacher" may have a particularly negative connotation for some. Students, like all of us, base their perceptions on their previous life experience, which is beyond our control. What is within our control is what we share about ourselves. It may be easy for students to lump you in with all other teachers if they experience you as someone who only conducts lessons, assigns homework, gives tests, and doles out grades. If, however, they see you as someone with a life outside of school filled with people, interests, hobbies, and interesting life experiences, you become not only a teacher, but a multifaceted person. It's much harder to keep you pigeonholed in that negative box when you are a three-dimensional person rather than a two-dimensional teacher. To begin the process of helping my students perceive me as a person rather than simply as an English teacher, I would give them a test on the first day of school. It was not a typical test, however. I would ask them to number their papers 1 through 20, and ask them questions like the following:

- How long have I been a teacher?
- What three things do I do for fun?
- What kinds of music do I enjoy?
- How many brothers and sisters do I have?
- Where did I grow up?

Sometimes, I would need to stop and explain that their grade on this test won't hurt them in any way (see what I mean about perceptions?). When the test was through, I would give them the correct answers. I got a kick out of listening to their guesses! It took just a few minutes to administer this "test," but would have been worth it even if it took three times as long. My students left the classroom that day with a much more complete perception of who I was as a person than they had when they entered the "English teacher's" room.

### Interest Inventory

Create an interest inventory for students to fill out at the beginning of the year. Use the information you gain about students' interests to connect and converse with them informally throughout the year. You might also, with students' permission, compile and publish the information you gain so that students can connect with other students who share their interests.

### Extracurricular Activities

One of the best ways to develop relationships with students is to attend extracurricular activities. Kids really appreciate teachers who attend their sporting events, plays, and concerts. It's a simple and effective way to show students that you care enough about them to invest some of your own personal time in something that is important to them. It also gives you something to talk to them about the next day at school.

## Journals

Using writing to learn content is an extremely effective strategy (see Learning Journals in Chapter 4). Sometimes, journaling can be a way to develop relationships. In a journal prompt, ask students their opinions about world, local, or school events. Or ask them to write about a family tradition regarding a particular holiday. Or use one of the topics for class meetings listed later in this chapter. The important thing is that you respond to their writing. You don't need to write a great deal, just a positive comment or two shows that you've read their entries, and that their thoughts and opinions count. This can be very time-consuming, so every week or two you might want to ask the students to mark with a star or an asterisk the journal entry or two that they'd like you to respond to.

## Lunch with the Teacher

Having lunch with your students is a great way to get to know each other. You could develop a formal system (a lottery, for example) for choosing your lunch companions or just do it informally. It is important though that you distribute this opportunity equitably.

## Other Ways to Develop Positive Relationships with Your Students

- Smile.
- Use humor appropriately.
- Be able to laugh at yourself.
- Provide adequate space for each student.
- Make sure students are always safe—physically and emotionally.
- Listen to students in and outside of the classroom.
- Attribute the ownership of ideas to those who initiated them. ("Dennis just made an interesting observation.")

*Caution:* This section has focused on befriending students, showing them you care about them and letting them learn appropriate information about you as a person. There is a big difference, however, between being a friend to your students and being their buddy. Your primary responsibility is still to be their teacher, making sure classroom behaviors are safe and appropriate and providing them with the knowledge and skills to become productive and responsible members of society. That means that as their friend you are firm about student responsibilities. A buddy, in contrast, overextends himself in sharing too much personal information or allowing students to shirk their responsibilities to themselves and others, often ignoring or sometimes even providing excuses for irresponsible behaviors. Sometimes in our exuberance to develop positive relationships with students, we can fall into the role of the buddy. Students generally have enough buddies; what they need from a teacher is a positive role model and a friend.

## Class Building

Although it is extremely important that students feel a sense of positive connection with and acceptance from their teachers, it may be even more critical that they experience a sense of belonging with their peers. Aside from the fact that all of us need to connect with our peers, today's social conditions seem to intensify this need. In the past, students came from stable, extended families and tightly knit neighborhoods and communities. Meeting the need for connection was relatively easy. Today, half of all students come from families touched by divorce, and families often move several times during a child's school years. Closely connected neighborhoods have given way to vast subdivisions, where many families hardly know the people right next door. Children, feeling this void, often attempt to fill it by gaining acceptance from their peers. Unfortunately, other children often do not freely provide acceptance. Having grown up watching situation comedies that base their humor on sarcasm, and in many cases, not having been taught positive social skills at home, children practice what they have experienced. As many teachers will attest, one result can be seen in classrooms that are full of putdowns, cruel humor, and various levels of violence.

It is unreasonable to expect the classroom teacher to single-handedly compensate for society's shortcomings. It takes a whole community working together to do that. What the classroom teacher can do, however, is intentionally create the conditions for students to connect and interact in positive ways, and to teach students the social skills that facilitate the process of connecting and working together. If you do this in your classroom, students will see and hear how positive interpersonal relations look and sound in at least one context, increasing the likelihood that they will take them when they walk out your door.

This section, which I call "class-building," will describe a number of ways you can help create a sense of positive interconnectedness, a team, a family in your classroom. As Jane Howard says, "Call it a clan, call it a network, call it a tribe, call it a family. Whatever you call it, whoever you are, you need one" (Harris, 2000, p. 62). As with all the other strategies in this book, most of them can be used with students of all ages. But you may need to modify them to be developmentally appropriate for the age group you work with.

## The Class Constitution

The class constitution, which some teachers like to refer to as a team agreement or class compact, is a set of behavioral guidelines set up by the students and the teacher together. Explained in detail in Chapter 4, the class constitution should be the prerequisite to any team-building efforts. It sets up behavioral expectations that ought to be

1. Reviewed before every team-building activity, especially early in the year.
2. Adhered to during team-building activities. All activity stops immediately if someone violates the constitution and only begins again when the party or parties who violated the behavioral expectations return to the agreed-upon behaviors. (If they do not, they are asked to sit out for the rest of the activity or until they choose to follow the guidelines they helped develop. As long as they do not disrupt the activity, they are allowed to stay in the room.)
3. Referred to after the activity as a way to help students learn to self-evaluate and as a way of keeping the constitution alive.

Students will see activities as more fun for everyone when they interact in positive ways.

## Manners 101

"*O tempora, O mores!* Oh, the times, Oh, the manners!" exclaimed Cicero (106–43 B.C., *In Catilinam*, I, 1). Over two thousand years later, the same cry, maybe more desperate, might be heard in almost any classroom in any school in America. Teachers with whom I work frequently complain about the lack of basic manners in their students. If the adage is true that "manners are the glue of our society," then at times it seems that our society is about to become unglued. Not only is it unpleasant to be around people with poor manners, rudeness often leads to arguments or worse. Many would argue that teaching manners is not the school's responsibility, that manners should be taught at home. I agree! But if that is not happening, we can either accept the lack of manners that our students demonstrate or do something about it in our classrooms. Out of the guidelines developed during the class constitution activity, one or two will invariably address respect or rudeness. Another prerequisite to working together as a class, especially if you are planning on doing any class-building or cooperative learning, is to address the topic of manners.

An excellent vehicle to teach manners is the class meeting. At the end of this chapter, I discuss many other topics and purposes for class meetings, as well as specific guidelines for holding them. You can use the following discussion questions to help your students understand the importance of good manners and to provide a format for teaching specific rules of basic etiquette:

- If an alien came down from outer space and wanted to learn good manners, what would you teach it?
- Who do you know who has very good manners? How do you feel about that person?
- What is the worst case of bad manners you've ever seen? What did you think of that person?
- How do you feel when someone is rude to you?
- How would you rate your own manners?

- "Thank you" is a phrase that shows good manners. List other polite words or phrases. Is it important for people to use these courtesies? Why?
- What would you consider bad table manners? Excellent table manners? Do they matter?
- Besides the dinner table, what other situations require manners?
- What would be good classroom manners? Bad classroom manners?
- What would be a polite way to interrupt someone if she was in the middle of a sentence?
- When someone treats you with respect, what do you think of him?
- What does shaking hands mean? When is it appropriate to shake hands?

Another way to teach manners in the classroom is to teach students the common words or phrases that people use to show courtesy and good manners. These phrases can be used in many situations: when students greet each other, when they part, when they want to encourage each other, when they disagree, or in many other circumstances. To begin, choose one phrase and have students practice it when you engage them in any of the class-building or cooperative learning activities. For example, if you use the Human Scavenger Hunt described in the next section, you might say to your students, "When you approach someone to ask if they fit a particular criteria, say 'Good morning.'" Following are phrases of standard etiquette that you might teach and have students practice:

- "Good morning."
- "Good afternoon."
- "Good to see you."
- "Thanks for the help."
- "Good suggestion."
- "What are your thoughts?"
- "Could I ask your opinion?"
- "I agree."
- "I disagree."
- "Talk to you later."

- "I enjoyed our talk."
- "Take care."

What are some other ways of being amenable you might teach your students? Maybe you could ask your students to develop a list.

### Human Scavenger Hunt

One of the first class-building strategies you might want to employ is the Human Scavenger Hunt. You begin by creating a list of characteristics that students in the class probably match, for example:

- Has been to another country.
- Has lived more than 200 miles from here.
- Has met someone famous.
- Has more than two brothers or sisters.
- Plays a musical instrument.
- Can speak a foreign language fluently.
- Has a cat or dog.
- Has an unusual pet.
- Has had his name or picture in the newspaper.
- Has won a prize (or award).
- Plays on a sports team.
- Loves to draw.

Give each student a sheet of paper with the characteristics, and tell them they have 10 minutes to get (1) as many different signatures from their classmates as possible, and (2) the details about the characteristics so that they can explain them to the class. After 10 minutes, stop the class, have them sit down and discuss what classmates learned about each other.

> TEACHER: Raise your hand if you found someone who's been to another country. Seth, who did you find?
>
> SETH: I found Cassandra. She's been to Mexico.
>
> TEACHER: Great! Cassandra, tell us something you liked about Mexico.

The Human Scavenger Hunt is a great way for the class and the teacher to learn interesting things about one another. English or language arts teachers might follow up this activity with a writing assignment about what students learned about their classmates.

## "Do You Know Your Neighbors?"

This is an activity I've used hundreds of times with students of all ages, from kindergartners through adults. It's been received with enthusiasm universally. Even my high school seniors, who try hard not to be enthusiastic about anything school-related (it's not cool, you know) used to beg me to play this game.

Start out with everyone sitting in a circle of chairs only, with no desks in the way. Make sure you clear all objects (purses, books, etc.) out of the circle. Stand in the middle of the circle and give the directions. There is no chair for you; there should be one chair fewer than the total number of people playing the game. Here are the directions you give:

1. "The person in the middle—and each of you will most likely have that honor—turns to someone in the group, says his or her name and asks that person, 'Do you know your neighbors?'" (Demonstrate: "Hector, do you know your neighbors?")

2. "The person I've asked says, 'Yes' and introduces the person to his left and to his right by first name only. (Demonstrate: Hector says, "Yes, this is Kirsten and this is Zander.") If you don't know their names, it's okay to ask."

3. "The person in the middle asks, 'Is there anyone else you'd like to know?' At this point the person being addressed says, 'Yes, I'd like to know someone who _____.' He fills in the blank with something he likes to do, something he likes to eat, a place he'd like to go, or something else he enjoys. For example, he might say, 'Yes, I'd like to know someone who likes chocolate.'"

4. "Once the person being addressed identifies something he likes, then he and everyone else who shares that interest stand and move quickly to another chair. One person will be left in the middle and the whole thing starts over again." Demonstrate:

TEACHER: Hector, is there anyone else you'd like to know?

HECTOR: Yes, I'd like to know someone who likes to play basketball.

(Everyone who likes basketball jumps up, frantically gets to another chair, and Samantha is left standing in the middle, laughing.)

"Do You Know Your Neighbors?" helps students find others with common interests, helps the teacher find topics to converse with their students about, and is a great energizer.

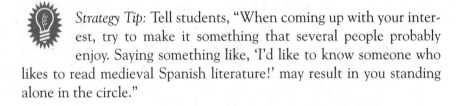 *Caution:* With kids, it's especially important to emphasize safety with this game. You might mention that this is not a contact sport, that chairs easily tip over, and that they keep that in mind when getting to their next seat.

*Strategy Tip:* Tell students, "When coming up with your interest, try to make it something that several people probably enjoy. Saying something like, 'I'd like to know someone who likes to read medieval Spanish literature!' may result in you standing alone in the circle."

### People Bingo

Another fun way to help students get acquainted and find commonalities is by playing People Bingo (Craigen & Ward, 1994). You'll need to make up a bingo sheet similar to the one in Figure 3.2. Have students put names of others who match them in the appropriate squares. When they have a straight line (or you might require two straight lines so the game will last longer), they yell, "Bingo!"

### Toilet Paper Introductions

This one usually starts out with a laugh. Have students sit in a circle. Take out a roll of toilet paper and pull off a few sheets. Then pass the roll to your right or left, saying only, "Take as much as you need." Some students

FIGURE 3.2

## People Bingo Card

| same eye color | same favorite sport | same class before this one | same favorite video game | same number of brothers |
|---|---|---|---|---|
| same number of sisters | same number of letters in first name | same color of shoes | same city of birth | same favorite ice cream |
| same favorite color | same number of aunts | **FREE** | same month of birth | same type of house |
| same favorite beverage | same color of hair | same favorite TV show | same favorite musical group | same favorite song |
| same kind of pet | same wake up time | wearing same color | same favorite movie | same height |

Source: Adapted from *What's This Got to Do with Anything?* by Jim Craigen and Chris Ward, © 1994 Visutronx. Used with permission by the publisher.

will take a single sheet; some will take a lot. After the roll has made it back to you, give the rest of the directions: "For each sheet of toilet tissue you took, share one bit of information about yourself." Demonstrate what kind of information by going first. For example, you might say, "I have two collies named Chester and Phoebe," or, "I love to go hiking, especially in the fall," or, "I really admire my friend Bob because he is such a good listener." For the students who took 50 sheets or so, you might let them off the hook by giving an upper limit of five or six bits of information.

*Variation:* You can modify this activity by using toothpicks, playing cards, or some other small objects instead of toilet paper.

## Food Discussions

This topic engages students of all ages. Have students jot down answers to the following questions, and then have them share their answers one at a time:

- What is one of your favorite foods?
- What is one of your least favorite foods?
- What is a food you used to dislike but now like?
- What is a food you used to like but now dislike?
- What is a food that a lot of people like, but you dislike?
- What is a food that a lot of people dislike, but you like?

This discussion can help students begin to see that we are all different and that, as with tastes in foods, different tastes in music, art, and so on are not bad—just different.

## Pairs of Hands

This activity is primarily designed for younger children (ages 7–11). In pairs, students trace each other's hand on a piece of paper. Then they share five pieces of information about themselves with each other and fill in each of the five fingers. Next, each pairing joins with another pairing, and each student introduces her partner and shares the five pieces of information she has learned.

## Bag o' Needs

Give each student a small brown paper bag. After teaching students about their five basic needs (survival, love and belonging, power, freedom, and fun) as explained in Chapter 1, give the students the following homework assignment: Bring in a photograph or small object from home that represents a way you meet each of your five basic needs. You might have a bag with some examples to provide a model for them. You might, for example, bring in a picture of your family for love and belonging, your diploma for power, a picture of yourself at the beach for freedom, a chess piece for fun, and a pair of boxing gloves for survival. If they aren't able to find something that fits in the bag, they can draw a picture of it on a 3" x 5" card and put that in the bag. The next day (or the next few days), the students can share their bags o' needs in pairs, small groups, or as a class.

## Class Web

This activity demonstrates actively and visually how the class is interdependent. All you need is a ball or skein of yarn. Start out by standing in a circle. Ask students to share information, such as

- A strength they bring to the classroom (sense of humor, ability to focus, etc.).
- Something they appreciate about another student.
- Something they learned about a classmate during a previous team-building activity.
- Something they learned during the current academic unit.

After each student shares his piece of information, have him hold onto his end of the yarn and toss the ball to another classmate across the circle. Demonstrate by sharing a piece of information and tossing the yarn across the circle to a student. The sharing and tossing continue until everyone in the circle is holding the yarn. It will look like a giant web. To process the activity:

- Ask what we learn from looking at the results of this activity.
- Have one student drop her piece and ask the group what effect this has on the web. Follow up by asking what behaviors would be analogous to "dropping the yarn" in the classroom.
- Have one student tug on the yarn and asking the group how that affects the web. Follow up by asking what would be analogous to "tugging the yarn" in the classroom.
- Ask the class what each individual can do to keep this web intact.

## True or False

Have each student make three statements about himself: two that are true and one that is false but plausible. In groups of four or five, have other students reach consensus on which statement is false (Craigen & Ward, 1994).

 *Variation:* Have the groups come up with two truths and a falsehood about their team, and have other teams guess which is false.

 *Strategy Tip:* The more outrageous the truths the better. This is a great way to find out some unusual information about each other.

## Baby, Look at You Now

Ask students to bring in baby pictures of themselves with permission from their parents. Then, have the students bring you their baby pictures and assign each one a number. Place the number on the back of their picture in pencil and keep a record for yourself. Give each member of the class a sheet with blanks next to each number and ask them to guess which picture goes with which student. After this activity, you might want to make a collage of the baby pictures and display them on a bulletin board for a while.

## Line-Ups

This activity helps students see that they each occupy a unique position in the classroom, while they learn a little more about their classmates (Kagan, 1994). Start out by announcing a criterion (e.g., age) by which students may vary (e.g., youngest to oldest). Students position themselves shoulder to shoulder along a continuum. Students then may pair or group up and discuss the topic. For example, "What do you like about being your age? What is the ideal age? Do you like when your birthday comes during the year?" Some line-up topics are

- Length of hair.
- Number of siblings.

Line-Ups appears with permission from Kagan Publishing & Professional Development from Spencer Kagan's book, *Cooperative Learning*. www.KaganOnline.com

- Height.
- Interest in _____.
- How far they live from school.
- How well organized their CDs (or socks, toys, videos) are.
- Alphabetical order by name (favorite sport, favorite color, favorite food).
- Date (birthday, favorite holiday, favorite month).
- Number (of buttons, pockets, shoe size).

## Corners

Using a general category of student interest, post three or four alternatives in different corners or different parts of the room (Kagan, 1994). Some suggestions for Corners topics are

- *Music:* country, classical, pop, punk, rap, metal, and trance.
- *Famous people:* George W. Bush, Bruce Willis, Britney Spears, Bret Favre, Jackie Chan, and Oprah Winfrey.
- *Vehicles:* pickup truck, SUV, electric car, sports car, motorcycle, snowmobile, and jet ski.
- *Buildings:* skyscraper, castle, log cabin, tent, penthouse apartment, and mansion.
- *Colors:* blue, green, red, yellow, brown, aqua, chartreuse, and forest green.
- *Places:* big city, suburb, country, small town, home, Mars, the moon, bottom of the ocean, West Coast, East Coast, beach, and mountains.
- *Birth Order:* oldest, youngest, middle child, and only child.
- *Metaphors:* babbling brook, rough seas, dark cave, lonely mountain top, calm lake, and flowing river.
- *Seasons:* summer, fall, winter, and spring.

Ask students which choice they most identify with. Give students 30–60 seconds to think; then have them write down their choice with a marker on a 3" x 5" card. (For nonreaders, put color-coded pictures on the signs. In this case, students put the color of their choice on their cards.) When you say "Go," the students hold their cards in front of them and go to the part of the room designated for their choice. When they go to their corner, they share with others who chose that corner what it is about that choice that attracted them. Then a spokesperson from each corner shares with the whole class what the people in his group said.

 *Variation:* The other groups paraphrase what they heard the spokesperson say.

 *Note:* The reason to have students write their choice down first is so that they will make this decision on their own and not just go to the corner their friend chooses.

## Personalogies

You'll be amazed at how this activity encourages your students' creativity and insight. Depending on your class size and the amount of time you have, you can do this in smaller groups (four to five) or as a whole class. Start out by placing a number of objects on a table or on the floor in the center of a circle, making sure you have more objects than the number of students in your class. The more variety the better: can opener, umbrella, crayon, box, string, clay, notepad, and so forth. Ask the students to choose any item about which they can say, "I am like this ____ because I . . ." and, "I am unlike this____ because I . . . ." Demonstrate what you want them to do: "I am like this ball of clay because I can easily adapt to new situations. I am unlike this ball of clay because I don't like people to manipulate me." Give them a minute to think and have them all come up at once to choose their item. All class members get to know each other in a new way.

 *Note:* You might want to suggest they pick a couple of objects at the beginning, just in case someone else gets to their first choice before they do.

## Animalogies

This variation of Personalogies can be used with any age but is generally better suited to younger students. Instead of placing objects on a table for the students to choose, use cards with pictures of animals. You can purchase animal cards very reasonably in the toy section of any department store. Just as in Personalogies, have the students pick a card about which they can say "I am like a ____ because I . . . " and "I am not like a ____ because I . . . . " Model this for the students: "I am like a turtle because sometimes I'm shy. I'm not like a turtle because I'm a fast runner."

*Variation:* You can also use this as a self-evaluation activity. Ask, "What animal best describes your attitude or behavior in school last year? What animal would you like to be more like this next year?"

*Note:* If you use this activity with older students, encourage them to be creative regarding the animals' characteristics. Instead of adhering to traditional views of animals (e.g., snakes are scary or sneaky), ask students to think more deeply about the animal before making their analogy. Demonstrate what you want them to do: "I'm like a snake because every once in a while I like to shed my old skin and start something new."

## Class Quilt

This activity is both a team builder and a great way of decorating your classroom. Set out as many different colors of construction paper and markers or crayons as possible. Have each student choose two pieces of paper of different colors. Then give the students the following directions:

- On one sheet, draw a picture of an important person (or people) or a picture of your pet(s).
- On the other sheet, draw a picture of yourself doing something you love to do, or something you are proud of accomplishing.

After they complete these drawings, ask the students to pair up and share their drawings. When they are finished sharing, have them connect their drawings by taping them together (tape on the back) so that they look like this:

Next, have pairs join with other pairs, share their drawings, and connect them together like this:

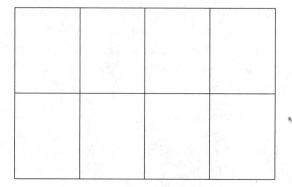

Continue to group students and connect drawings until you have a whole class quilt. If you end up with an irregular figure, you can add sheets of construction paper to make it a regular rectangle. These sheets might include

- The date the quilt was made.
- The class name (Ms. Shaheen's 9th-Period Social Studies Class).
- The students' signatures.

This activity helps students discover common interests, celebrate their uniqueness, take ownership in decorating their classroom, and see their interconnection in a concrete way.

## Mix-Freeze-Pair

This is a structure Kagan describes in *Cooperative Learning* (1994) that can be used as both a class-building strategy and a cooperative learning tool. Have students stand up and randomly move around the room while you play some energetic music. Encourage them to dance around the room if they so desire. When the music stops, they are to freeze. Then direct them to turn to the nearest person; this will be their partner for the activity. Ask them to raise their hand if they do not have a partner, so that those who don't immediately get in a pair aren't left out. If there is an odd number, simply create one triad. If you don't have music, just have them move around until you give a signal (lights off and on, clap hands, etc.). Once they are in a pair, give them a topic to discuss, give them a time limit (1–2 minutes), and repeat the activity, making sure they pair with a different person each time the music stops. Here are some topics that lend themselves to Mix-Freeze-Pair:

- Your favorite musical group, rapper, or singer.
- Your favorite kind of music.
- Someone who is important to you.
- Something you do for fun.
- Something you are good at.
- Your favorite meal.
- Your favorite dessert.
- A food that you hate.
- Someone you admire or respect.
- Something funny that happened to you.
- An embarrassing moment.
- Your favorite joke (appropriate).
- Your favorite movie.
- Your favorite song.
- The most memorable scene from an action movie.
- The best vacation or weekend you can remember.
- Your favorite movie star.
- Your favorite television show.
- A name you'd choose if you had to choose a new first name.
- Something few people know about you.
- Your greatest strength and one of your weaknesses.

Mix-Freeze-Pair appears with permission from Kagan Publishing & Professional Development from Spencer Kagan's book, *Cooperative Learning*. www.KaganOnline.com

- A name you'd never give to your child.
- A place you'd love to visit.
- What you'd do with a million dollars.
- What kind of gift you would give the world.
- Someone from history you'd like to meet.
- Someone you'd like to meet who is alive today.
- Something for which you are grateful.

## Trading Cards

This is one variation of Mix-Freeze-Pair. Give each student a 3" x 5" card with one of the preceding topics (or another) on it. Follow the previously given directions for getting into pairs. Once in pairs, have them answer the question on their card, trade cards, and get into another pair.

 *Note:* In Mix-Freeze-Pair and Trading Cards, you might add this additional structure: Once in pairs, have students determine who is Partner A and who is Partner B. Partner A talks for one minute on the given topic, then Partner B talks. If you are also trying to develop listening skills, have the students summarize what they heard their partner share before they talk about themselves.

## Uncommon Commonalities

This activity, discussed in Christian and Tubesing (1997), helps students discover many things they have in common with others in a short time. Pair students at random and tell them that they have five minutes to find the most unusual thing that they have in common. In the process of doing this, they will talk about dozens of things they like, dislike, places they've been, people they've met, and other life experiences, many of which they will have in common. Finally, they will discover some unusual commonality. For example, they might discover that they both

- Love peanut butter and baloney sandwiches.
- Have been camping in Pennsylvania in January.
- Were at the same concert.
- Dislike catsup.
- Had chicken pox when they were in 4th grade.

- Have pet iguanas.
- Were afraid of dust bunnies when they were little.

You can never predict the uncommon commonalities your students will discover. You might even have the class vote on the most uncommon commonality (no voting for your own). One thing I can predict: There will be lots of surprises and lots of laughs when you play Uncommon Commonalities.

## Theme Days

One way to develop a class identity is to have a theme day once a month when students dress according to a particular theme or idea. Some possible themes include

- Hat Day (or Silly Hat Day),
- Dress Up Day,
- '70s Day,
- Future Day,
- Medieval Day,
- Color Day (Blue Day, Black and White Day, etc.),
- Slippers Day,
- Rock Star Day, and
- Sports Day

The themes could be just for fun, related to a national holiday, or tied to a concept or topic you are studying in class.

## Predictions and Perceptions

This activity, explained by Mel Silberman in *Active Learning: 101 Strategies to Teach Any Subject* (1996), is a good one to do after the students have gotten to know each other a little bit and have had some practice using the class constitution (see Chapter 4). First, divide the class into groups of four, making sure students who know each other well are in different groups. Tell students that their job is to predict how each person in their group will answer certain questions you have prepared for them. Some of those questions can include the following:

- What is your favorite music?
- How many siblings do you have, and where are you in the sibling order?
- Are your parents strict or lenient?
- What chores do you have at home?
- What job do you want to have as an adult?
- When you're on your own, do you want to live in the city, the country, or the suburbs?
- What's your favorite snack food?

You can also use many of the topics from Mix-Freeze-Pair.

Next, have the small groups select one person as the first focus person. Urge group members to be as specific as possible in their predictions about this person. As they guess, ask the focus person to give no indication of the accuracy of the predictions attempted. When they finish their predictions, have the focus person reveal the answer to each question about herself. Then have the groups move on to the next person.

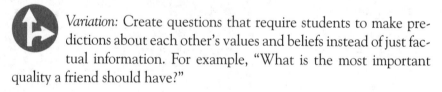

*Variation:* Create questions that require students to make predictions about each other's values and beliefs instead of just factual information. For example, "What is the most important quality a friend should have?"

This activity demonstrates that even when students think they know each other, their perceptions are never completely accurate. Their classmates are complex individuals who always have a few surprises up their sleeves.

### Group Résumé

This activity works best when students have spent some time working together and know each other. It is also "especially effective if the résumé is geared to the subject matter you are teaching" (Silberman, 1996, p. 38). First divide the class into groups of three or four. Tell the class that together they display a wide variety of skills and talents. Explain that one of the best ways to identify and celebrate these resources is to write a group résumé. Give all the groups colored markers and a big piece of newsprint, and ask them to create a poster to display their résumé. They might want to include information about

- Educational background;
- Knowledge and skills about the class content;
- Job experience;
- Positions held;
- Accomplishments; or
- Hobbies, talents, and travel.

Show the class a model résumé to help them understand the assignment. A résumé for an 11th grade English class might look like the one in Figure 3.3. When the students are finished, have them share their résumés and celebrate their combined resources with the whole class.

### Class Mission Statement

Creating a class mission statement builds the class as a team and gives students a shared purpose, such as

> OUR MISSION: To achieve our personal best while working and playing in a supportive and challenging learning environment.

To create a mission statement for your class, follow these steps:

1. Divide the class into small groups of three or four, making sure each group has a *leader* to keep the group on task; a *recorder* to write down the group's ideas; and a *reporter* to report the group's ideas to the class.
2. Pose the questions: What is the purpose of this class? What do you want to accomplish in this class this year?
3. Give the group five to ten minutes to brainstorm their ideas.
4. Go from group to group and get one idea from the reporter in each group. Record a class list on the board, a flip chart, or on the overhead.

FIGURE 3.3

Example of Group Résumé

# Pencils for Hire

*Peer Editors Extraordinaire*
(Shania, Sean, Brianna, Ramone)

### Objective

Desire experience with editing creative and expositive writing

### Qualifications

- 40 years of combined public school education
- All *B*s or better on class writing this year
- Knowledge of
  - Subject/verb agreement
  - Punctuation
  - Passive and active voice
  - Spelling
  - MLA guidelines for writers of research papers
- Friendly, courteous, and tactful
- Hobbies include reading, basketball, sunbathing, and snacking

5. Once you've recorded all the ideas, pare them down with the class by eliminating those that are repetitive and those that class members do not agree on.

6. As a group, try to develop a sentence or two that incorporates all their suggestions.

7. Check for consensus.

8. Post the class mission statement in a prominent place in the classroom. You might include it on future class assignments, tests, letters home, and other items.

## Cooperative Learning

Taking time with class-building activities is an investment, not only in building and maintaining positive relationships for their own sake, but also in preparing students for one of the most effective teaching strategies there is: cooperative learning. In their comprehensive book on educational practices, *Research on Educational Innovations*, Ellis and Fouts state, "Of all the educational innovations we have reviewed . . . [which include brain-based learning, multiple intelligences, learning styles, direct instruction, mastery learning, among others], cooperative learning has the best and largest empirical base" (1997, p. 173). Three of the most well-known experts on cooperative learning, brothers David and Roger Johnson and their sister Edythe Johnson Holubec, add further support to the practice of cooperative learning in their book *Circles of Learning:* "Over 375 experimental studies on achievement have been conducted of the past 90 years. A meta-analysis of all studies indicates that cooperative learning results in significantly higher achievement and retention than do competitive and individualistic learning" (1993, p. 2:16).

Not only does cooperative learning result in higher achievement and greater long-term retention of what is learned, it also tends to result in

- Higher-level reasoning (critical thinking);
- Process gain (more new ideas, strategies, and solutions generated);
- Transfer of what is learned from one situation to another;

- Positive attitudes toward the subject being studied; and
- Time on task.

The research supporting the use of cooperative learning is so persuasive that you might ask why every teacher isn't using it. The answer lies in understanding the difference between effective cooperative learning strategies and "group work." Many teachers, having the best intentions, group students together, give them a task, maybe even assign some roles, and set them to work. These teachers eventually give up on what they believe is cooperative learning because

- The students were off task,
- One student did all the work while the others sat back,
- The students started bickering amongst themselves, or
- Parents complained that their child's grade shouldn't depend on others' performance.

These are all valid complaints, and as a novice teacher I experienced them myself. What I did not yet understand was that I was not implementing cooperative learning; I was engaging my students in group work. As Ellis and Fouts suggest, "to do it [cooperative learning] well, takes training" (1997, p. 173).

Cooperative learning must be structured in ways that intentionally avoid arguments, keep students on task, encourage individual accountability, and are assessed fairly. If you have started the year with effective class-building strategies, you have already developed the foundation for effective cooperative learning. This section will describe basic structures that you can use in any subject area, first with pairs working together and then with teams of three and four.

## Cooperative Pairs

Before students can work together, they have to get together. One pitfall is students' gravitating toward the same individual each time they're asked to work with someone. To avoid this, explain that they will be working with a number of different groups and pairs during the year. Sometimes they'll work with good friends, but occasionally they may work with partners they may not have chosen on their own. You might discuss how this is like the real world, and that it is important to learn to work with all kinds of people. Tell them that if they are paired or grouped with people who would not be their first choice, they should do their best and usually sooner than later, the groupings will change. Having this discussion will minimize the inevitable whining that often accompanies pairing students. Another strategy to avoid complaints is to use a variety of ways to pair students, such as the following ideas that that have worked for me.

**Mix-Freeze-Pair.** See the preceding section on Class Building for a description of this activity.

**Opposite Cards.** Make up a bunch of 3" x 5" cards of opposites that go together in pairs (e.g., Hot/Cold, Big/Small, Over/Under). Give your students the cards and tell them to find the person holding the opposite card when you say "Go!" For example, if Miguel is holding a card that says "Up," he is looking for the person who has the "Down" card.

*Variations*: Use pairs of cards that have either the first and last name of celebrities, famous historical figures, or cartoon characters on them. Or use Opposite Cards to simultaneously review content: a term or vocabulary word on one card, and the definition on the other.

**Pacing Partners.** Have students stand up and face any direction they like. Make sure they are facing a variety of directions. Have them take a certain number of paces in whatever direction they are facing. After they do that, have them turn to the nearest person. That is their partner. Have anyone who still does not have a partner raise her hand, look around, and find another person whose hand is up or join one pair as a triad.

**Appointment Book Partners.** At the beginning of a unit, hand out a sheet that looks like a page from an appointment book (see Figure 3.4). Give the students five minutes to get a different name next to each time. Remind them to make sure their names go in the same time slots on their partners' sheets. For example, if John puts Sue's name next to 9:00, Sue must put John's name under 9:00 on her sheet. When you need them to get with a partner for an activity, you just randomly select a time and say, for example, "Now, sit with your 11:00 partner." This method saves lots of time.

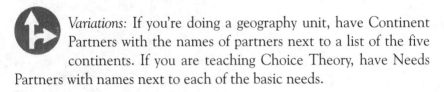 *Variations:* If you're doing a geography unit, have Continent Partners with the names of partners next to a list of the five continents. If you are teaching Choice Theory, have Needs Partners with names next to each of the basic needs.

**Door Cards.** Dave Quackenbush, a social studies teacher at Corning West High School in Corning, New York, frequently uses this strategy in his class. Dave has tables of four in his classroom. Each table has a letter on it and each seat a number. As his students enter his classroom, he hands them each a card with their designated seat (e.g., B3) next to the partner or partners they will be working with in pairs or cooperative groups on that day.

---

FIGURE 3.4

**Appointment Book**

9:00    _____

10:00   _____

11:00   _____

12:00   _____

1:00    _____

2:00    _____

3:00    _____

4:00    _____

---

Using a variety of pairing strategies adds novelty to the classroom. Some of the previously described strategies are truly random (e.g., Mix-Freeze-Pair, Pacing Partners), whereas others seem to be random but allow the teacher some control in who works with whom (e.g., Opposite Cards). To move from these pairs to a cooperative group of four, you might use a variation of some of the previously described strategies or simply have the pairs find another pair to work with.

## Activities for Pairs or Teams

Once students are in a cooperative pair or group, you can use the following structured activities to help them stay on task, work together effectively, and remain accountable individually.

**Brains Storming.** As they say, two heads are better than one. And two brains can storm more ideas than one. Give each pair of students a Brains Storming sheet, like the one in Figure 3.5. (You will be able to find images of brains in many clip-art software packages.) Then give them a topic to brainstorm, assign a recorder, and have them go back and forth generating ideas and writing them right on the brain image. You can use this activity to uncover prior knowledge about a particular topic, develop ideas for writing assignments or projects, identify ways they could apply content, solve a problem, or in any other situation where you want to generate a lot of ideas in a short time.

**Inside–Outside Circle.** This extremely flexible pairs structure, discussed by Kagan (1994), can be used in a variety of ways in almost any classroom. The only requirement is enough space. The steps of Inside/Outside Circle are the following:

1. Have students count off by twos.
2. Direct the "ones" to stand in a circle.
3. Once they have arranged themselves in a circle, ask them to turn around so that they are facing out.
4. Direct the "twos" to face the "ones," so that they create an outer circle.
5. Give the students a direction such as, "Shake hands with the person you are facing and say 'Good morning!' "

Inside–Outside Circle appears with permission from Kagan Publishing & Professional Development from Spencer Kagan's book, *Cooperative Learning.* www.KaganOnline.com

---

**FIGURE 3.5**

**"Brains Storming"**

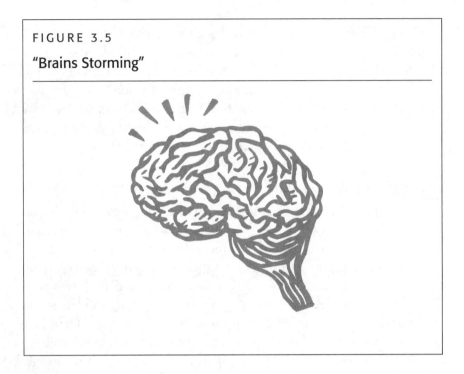

---

6. Give the students a question or problem to discuss and a time
   parameter. For example: "For the next two minutes, discuss everything you know about the Civil War."

7. After the time limit is up, direct them to shake hands again and to
   say, "Nice talking to you."

8. Direct one of the circles to move to the right or left by a certain
   number of people. For example: "Outer circle, move three people
   to your right. Please say 'Hi' to the people you walk past."

9. Either give them the same questions or problem, or ask them to
   discuss something different.

10. Repeat steps 5–10, as needed.

The Inside/Outside Circle can be used in many ways:

- As an icebreaker or team builder, giving questions like those listed
  previously in this chapter under Mix-Freeze-Pair.

- To help students discover prior knowledge about a particular topic before holding a large-group discussion.

- As a drill-and-practice activity. For example, give each student a different term or vocabulary word and its definition. During Inside/Outside Circle, have students check the understanding of the person opposite them and then rotate one of the circles. You might even have students switch cards with the person opposite them after each rotation.

- As a review. Each prompt could be to ask the students to review what they remember about a specific aspect of a lesson or unit they are about to be assessed on.

- As a listening exercise. Have the inner circle speak first for a minute or two about a particular topic. The outer circle can't say anything. Then have the members of the outer circle summarize what they heard their partners say. Then have the inner-circle students give the outer-circle students feedback on how accurate and complete their summaries were. Then have "ones" and "twos" switch roles.

**Pairs Discuss.** This activity, described by Johnson, Johnson, and Holubec (1993), is a great follow-up to teacher-guided practice on a particular skill. Once the teacher gives an assignment, partners take turns answering a question or doing a problem while the other partner coaches and gives feedback. Once they've done that two or three times, both do the work, stopping after each two or three questions or problems and checking their answers (and the thinking behind them) with each other.

**Pick a Card, Any Card.** This cooperative learning activity encourages total student engagement and accountability. You will need two sets of regular playing cards. Divide the class into teams of four and give each student on each team a card of a different suit. After assigning the teams a task (hold a discussion, brainstorm some ideas, solve a problem, etc.), pull a card at random out of the deck. The student in each group who holds the same suit as the card you pulled reports her team's ideas or answer.

*Variation:* Make sure each member of each team has the same number or face cards (one team has all the aces, one all the threes, etc.). When you pull your card out of the other deck, the value of the card selects the first team to share (the Jacks, for example), and the suit selects the member of each team who will report to the class.

*Note:* You can also use this strategy to assign roles. For example, hearts will be the facilitators; spades will be the recorders; diamonds will report to the class; and clubs will be in charge of materials.

**Jigsaw.** As teachers well know, the best way to learn something is to teach it to others. This cooperative learning activity requires students to do just that. These are the steps:

1. Identify content that could be divided into relatively equal meaningful segments.
2. Identify the number of segments to be learned and place that number of students in each learning team.
3. Assign each person in the learning team a different segment of the material to learn and give them time to study.
4. Students then meet in expert groups to make sure they have a good grasp of their specific segment of the material and to discuss how they will teach their portion to their learning teams.
5. Students return to their learning teams and teach the material they have become experts on.
6. Ensure individual accountability by some means, possibly by using Pick a Card, Any Card or having a traditional quiz.

*Notes:* If the Jigsaw strategy is new to your students, start out with simple content. They will first need to learn the process before combining it with complex content. Also, after their Jigsaw experience, provide students with an opportunity to discuss how they worked as groups, what skills were needed to be successful, what worked well, and what they might do differently next time to improve the process (Johnson, Johnson, & Holubec, 1993).

**Graffiti.** This cooperative learning activity has the added benefit of allowing students to get out of their seats and move around the room. You might use Graffiti to have students offer solutions to problems, list what they think they know about a topic, review what they have learned in a particular unit, use vocabulary in sentences of their own, or generate ideas (Rutherford, 1998). Here are the steps:

1. Write several topics, problems, and sentences on pieces of large chart paper and post them around the room.
2. Divide the students into groups of three to five, and assign each group to one of the pieces of chart paper.
3. Give students enough time to accomplish the task at their station.
4. Have students write their answers or ideas on the chart paper.
5. After the time limit is up, give the students a signal to rotate to the next chart and repeat until all the groups have responded to all the charts.

**Formations.** This cooperative strategy incorporates movement, which benefits the kinesthetic learner and gives all students a break from sitting at their desks or tables all day (Kagan, 1994). The object of Formations is for each cooperative group to create a physical representation of a word, an object, or a process that they have learned about in class. The steps of Formations are as follows:

1. Divide the class into appropriately sized groups, depending on what you are hoping the groups to form.
2. Give each group a slip of paper explaining what they are to represent with a formation.
3. Give groups a designated amount of time to develop their formation.
4. Have groups present their formations to the rest of the class.
5. If the formations are incomplete or unclear, ask the class to offer suggestions that would improve the formation.

Formations can be used with students of all ages. The only variable would be the complexity of the idea, process, or thing you would ask

Formations appears with permission from Kagan Publishing & Professional Development from Spencer Kagan's book, *Cooperative Learning.* www.KaganOnline.com

your students to represent physically. Some ideas for formations include the following:

- *Letters or numbers:* Have the students form the shape of letters they're learning about.
- *Spelling:* Students would use their bodies to spell out a term or vocabulary word.
- *Geography:* Students form a map of a state, country, or continent.
- *Math:* Students represent an equation or a math process ($\frac{1}{2}$ x 6 = 3), or students use their bodies to create geometric shapes.
- *Science:* Students represent the solar system or show how the earth rotates around the sun. Or students physically depict the circulatory system or respiration.
- *Technology:* Students represent technological inventions.

**All Hands on Deck.** This strategy, explained by Paula Rutherford (1998), promotes participation by all students, focuses students on a topic to be studied, and helps uncover students' prior knowledge about the topic to be studied. The process is as follows:

1. Post chart paper that lists subtopics of the topic to be studied around the room, and give examples of ideas that might be included on each chart. For example, if a high school social studies class was studying the topic of the social conditions of the 1960s, subtopics might include popular music, television shows, recreational activities, famous slogans of the time, celebrities, famous historical or cultural events, and more. You might give students some examples of popular music (The Beatles, Jimi Hendrix) or famous historical or cultural events (The Bay of Pigs, Woodstock) to get them started.

2. Give each team of four students a stack of index cards with the same subtopics written on the posted chart paper.

3. Students divide the index cards equally among the members of the team.

4. Give students a designated amount of time (one to two minutes) to brainstorm ideas about the subtopics, with the expectation that each student will contribute at least one idea per card.

5. When the time elapses, have the students pass their cards to the team member to their left and repeat Step 4. Continue circulating the cards until all team members have written on each card.

6. A designated reporter on each team reads one contribution for the selected chart on the wall in round-robin fashion while the teacher or a student records the ideas. When one chart is completed, move to the next.

 *Variation:* Provide teams with pieces of paper with the subtopics printed on the top, and give each student a stack of sticky notes. Students write their ideas on the sticky notes and post them on the paper. Large-group sharing can be done by posting the sticky notes on the chart paper and conducting a walking tour of the charts.

*Note:* To encourage individual accountability, provide students with different color writing implements or sticky notes (Rutherford, 1998).

**I Have–Who Has.** This activity is a great drill-and-practice activity or one you can use for review. Students stand in a circle. The teacher gives each student a 3" x 5" card. On one side of the card is a term; on the other side is a definition of a term that appears on another card in the circle. Place a green dot on the definition side of one card. The student with the green dot starts by saying, "Who has . . . ?" and reads his definition. The student who has the card with that term that matches that definition says, "I have . . . " and reads her term. She goes on, saying, "Who has . . . ?" and reads her definition. A typical exchange can go like this one:

> ANN: Who has "a quadrilateral with four equal sides"?
>
> SIMON: I have "a square." Who has "a figure with three equal sides"?
>
> TREVOR: I have "an equilateral triangle." Who has . . .?

These exchanges continue until all of the definitions have been read and matched with the correct term. If the student matches his term incorrectly, the group is encouraged to discuss the answer.

**Inquiring Minds.** This process helps students focus on a class reading assignment, learn important questioning skills, and engage higher-level thinking skills. Have students work in teams of three or four engaging in the following process:

1. The Reader reads a section of the assigned text. (The length of the section would be developmentally appropriate, maybe a paragraph or two.)

2. The Inquiring Mind writes down a question on an index card, using one of the question starters (see Figure 3.6), and passes it to the Answerer.

3. The Answerer reads the question aloud and answers it. If he cannot answer the question on his own, he may "phone the Friend" if there is a fourth team member or ask for coaching from the group.

4. The Friend or group helps the Answerer.

---

FIGURE 3.6

## Question Starters

| | | |
|---|---|---|
| Who ...? | What ...? | Where ...? |
| Who might ...? | What was ...? | Where might ... |
| Who would ...? | What were ...? | Where could ...? |
| Who seemed ...? | What if ...? | Where do ...? |
| Which ... ? | What could ...? | Where would you find ...? |
| Which might ...? | What might ...? | Where might you look ...? |
| Which could ...? | What facts ...? | Where in the textbook ...? |
| Which were ...? | What can ...? | Where do you see ...? |
| How ...? | Why ...? | Can ...? |
| How might ...? | Why might ...? | Can you list ...? |
| How would ...? | Why do ...? | Can you name ...? |
| How do ...? | Why should ...? | Can you explain ...? |
| How is ...? | Why are ...? | Can you describe ...? |

5. When the team agrees that the answer is correct, the Answerer writes it down on the index card.

6. The roles shift to the left one person, and the process repeats until the reading assignment is complete.

You might then use the questions that the students develop for other activities or for the unit test.

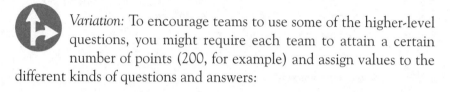 *Variation:* To encourage teams to use some of the higher-level questions, you might require each team to attain a certain number of points (200, for example) and assign values to the different kinds of questions and answers:

- Knowledge—5 points
- Comprehension—10 points
- Application—15 points
- Analysis—20 points
- Synthesis—25 points
- Evaluation—30 points

You could then use the questions that the students develop for other activities or for the unit test.

**Team or Pair Projects.** One way to assess students' learning at the end of a study unit is to allow them to work together as a team. Before the teams begin on their projects, it is essential that they understand what specific knowledge or skills their project must demonstrate. It is your job to clarify your expectations. Next, it is important that they demonstrate a clear understanding of the characteristics of a quality team or pair project. I'd recommend enlisting the students to identify these criteria. Using a combination of the criteria you've listed and those that the students identified, you can develop a checklist to assess their group projects. Figure 3.7 is a checklist that my 12th grade English students and I developed at the end of a unit on John Gardner's novel *Grendel*.

We decided that the criteria listed under 1 would determine 60 percent of the project's grade, and the criteria listed under 2 would determine 40 percent. After each presentation, the class and I would rate the presentation by scoring each criterion from 0 to 5 (5 being best). Each

---

**FIGURE 3.7**

## Checklist of criteria to assess group project

1. The project will demonstrate an understanding of
   __ The literal level of the novel (the plot).
   __ How John Gardner uses literary elements such as point of view, character development, character change, symbolism, and plot resolution to develop the novel's theme(s).
   __ One of the major themes of the novel.
2. A quality team project will
   __ Be well organized.
   __ Engage the audience, intellectually or actively.
   __ Be delivered with appropriate volume and clarity of expression.
   __ Demonstrate equal participation by each member of the team.
   __ Be 20 to 30 minutes in length.

---

student received two grades: a group grade and an individual grade. The individual grade was based solely on their work as a team member. This grade was determined partially by me—based on my observation of how they worked during the class time they were provided—and partially by the members of the team—who rated themselves and their peers on their performance as team members. Their rating sheets included the following criteria:

1. Attended team meetings.
2. Carried out team responsibilities.
3. Treated other team members with courtesy.
4. Communicated effectively with other team members.

I felt that using this system was the fairest way to allow them to do group projects and still have individual accountability.

Whether you use a system similar to mine or develop one of your own, the important thing is for students to know at all times what is expected of them. I also recommend that you provide adequate class time for students to work on their group projects. That doesn't mean that 100 percent of the team preparation time needs to be during class time. Students should be encouraged to divide the labor and do some work individually outside the classroom. Here are some examples of group projects:

- In math, students develop and present a problem that takes a series of calculations to solve.
- In science, students present an experiment they carried out, the data they collected, and the conclusions they reached.
- In social studies, students write a group Teenage Declaration of Independence, having all the components of the 1776 United States document.
- In English, students act out a scene from a novel or short story and discuss its implications.
- In foreign language, students demonstrate how a particular culture or language has influenced our culture or language.

There are literally dozens of ways students can demonstrate their understanding of subject area content. For more suggestions, see the list of Alternative Assessment Ideas in Chapter 5.

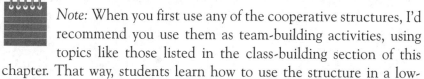 *Note:* When you first use any of the cooperative structures, I'd recommend you use them as team-building activities, using topics like those listed in the class-building section of this chapter. That way, students learn how to use the structure in a low-stress setting and build good relationships with their partner or members of their team. Once they have successfully used the structure in this way, then engage students in content-related discussions or problem-solving activities.

In addition, many of the structures listed in the class-building section of this chapter can be easily modified to relate to content. Those that especially lend themselves to content-related topics are Line-Ups, Class Web, True or False, Corners, Mix-Freeze-Pair, and Trading Cards.

## The Class Meeting

The class meeting, both a class-building and cooperative learning structure, is such an effective classroom procedure that it deserves a section of it own. Glasser has been a proponent of class meetings since his *Schools Without Failure* was published in 1969. He says starting as soon as "children enter kindergarten [they should] discover that each class is a working, problem-solving [and learning] unit and that each student has both individual and group responsibilities. Responsibility for learning and for behaving so that learning is fostered is shared among the entire class" (1969, p. 123). The regular use of the class meeting encourages this kind of responsibility and has many other benefits.

The ideas and suggestions about class meetings come from Glasser's *Schools Without Failure*, from workshops presented by Al Katz, a senior faculty member of the William Glasser Institute, and from my own experience. Although class meetings are explained in this chapter, which focuses on the love and belonging need, the class meeting strategy is also an extremely effective way to help students meet their other needs. First, setting and adhering to the guidelines for class meetings ensures a safe and orderly environment, enabling students to meet their survival need. Second, speaking and being listened to are effective ways of meeting the need for power. Third, during a class meeting, students are free to express themselves as well as free from the daily class routine. And finally, most students think class meetings are fun! See Figure 3.8 for some guidelines on running an effective class meeting.

### Purposes of Class Meetings

Class meetings have many different purposes, including

- *Developing a trusting, supportive environment.* The first several class meetings you hold should simply teach the process of holding a class meeting, using topics that help class members learn about one another in a safe, encouraging way.
- *Solving class problems.* A great way to learn problem-solving skills is to apply them to real class problems. Maybe some members of the class think that you have not provided them with enough class

time to prepare for a presentation. Or, maybe there has been a rash of put-downs in class lately. Or, the class decides it wants to go on a field trip and doesn't have enough money to pay for it. These are all opportunities to hold a class meeting to solve the problem, while practicing critical-thinking skills.

- *Teaching clear thinking.* It is impossible to talk without thinking, though that sometimes doesn't seem to be the case. But, speaking and writing require higher-order thinking skills. By listening to what students say, we can often see any problems in their logic. By

---

**FIGURE 3.8**

## Some Guidelines for Class Meetings

---

1. Sit in a circle with no furniture in the way (optional).
2. Set ground rules every time:
   a. The person speaking must keep to the here and now.
   b. One person speaks at a time. No interruptions or side conversations.
   c. The person speaking must use "I statements."
   d. The focus is on listening to other group members; no other activity is acceptable.
   e. Everyone who wants to may participate.
   f. No put-downs, verbal or non-verbal

3. Use a ball of some sort or a "talking stick" to designate the speaker.
4. Be nonjudgmental, but be directive when necessary.
5. Keep the length of the meeting developmentally appropriate. (Length of meeting in minutes = Age of the participants x 2)
6. Hold meetings at regularly scheduled times, but hold problem-solving meetings when necessary. Anyone in the class can recommend holding a problem-solving meeting.

demonstrating clear thinking and encouraging students frequently to practice, we can teach them to think and speak more clearly. One of my rules for class meetings is that students must back up their opinions with supporting details, facts, and examples. They are encouraged to say things such as: "I agree with _____ because . . . " or "I disagree with _____ because . . . ." This not only helps them develop their ability to construct support, but it also teaches them to disagree with someone respectfully.

- *Teaching social skills.* Class meetings provide lots of opportunities to learn, discuss, and practice effective social skills and good manners. Sometimes, they may be the topic of the class meeting. Other times, they may just come up as group interaction dictates.

- *Building student confidence, especially in verbal areas.* As Jerry Seinfeld once remarked: "Public speaking is the number one fear in America. Death is number two. So, if you're going to be at a funeral, you're better off in the casket than doing the eulogy." It is true that many people panic when faced with an audience. Safe, supportive class meetings are a great way to help students overcome a fear of speaking in public, something they will inevitably be required to do at some time in their lives.

- *Bringing relevance to the classroom.* One of the best ways for students to deepen their learning about a particular concept or process is for them to see how it relates to their lives. After a lesson or unit, the right kind of questions posed during a class meeting might bring the unit to life in a way no other strategy could.

- *Helping determine the learning needs of your students.* Using a KWL (Know-Want-Learned, see Chapter 4) strategy during a class meeting can help you discover your students' prior knowledge about a particular topic. Then you can determine where to start, or what skills or prerequisite information you might need to teach. A class meeting can also be used to determine whether your students are ready for a particular formal assessment or if you need to reteach a particular piece to certain students, maybe in a different mode than you previously used.

## Types of Meetings

**Class-Building Meetings.** I recommend using the class-building meeting format before trying to use class meetings for any other purposes. This practice will serve three purposes: (1) helping the class get to know each other, (2) helping lower students' anxiety about speaking in front of the class, and (3) helping students learn the process of class meetings before using them for other purposes.

For the first few class-building meetings, you might start out with a "whip," a structure in which you quickly go around the circle and every student fills in the blank of a starter sentence with a simple word or phrase. Even shy students will be more likely to respond if all that is called for is a short, simple response. Whips are also good ways to share a lot of information in a short time. The discussion moves very quickly, whipping around the circle, hence the name. Some topics for a whip include

- Someone who is important to you;
- Someone you'd like to meet who is alive today;
- Someone from history you'd like to meet;
- Your favorite musical group, rapper, or singer;
- Something you do for fun;
- Something you are good at;
- Your favorite song;
- Your favorite main course;
- Your favorite dessert;
- A food that you dislike;
- Your favorite movie;
- Your favorite movie star;
- Your favorite television show;
- A name you'd choose if you had to choose a new first name;
- Your greatest strength and one of your weaknesses;
- A name you'd never give to your child;
- A place you'd love to visit;
- What you'd do with a million dollars;
- If you could give the world a gift; or
- Something for which you are grateful.

Once students feel comfortable in the circle, you might want to develop questions that require the students to define, personalize, and use higher-level thinking skills regarding concepts in your content area or other topics, such as Manners, Happiness, Rules, Tolerance, Adolescence, Culture, The Role of a Parent, Art, Friendship, Fairness, Freedom, Criticism, Responsibility, Money, Love, Independence, Quality of Life, Work, The Purpose of Education, Dreams, Humor, Time, Relationships, Mortality, Marriage, Justice, Citizenship, Respect, Wealth and Poverty, Sharing, Equality, and Decisions.

In addition, the following questions can help students discuss topics that relate to emotional intelligence self-regulation and relationship maintenance, both of which are important issues in any classroom or school:

- Tell about something funny that happened to you.
- Tell your favorite (appropriate) joke.
- What is something few people know about you?
- What is the best vacation or weekend you can remember?
- What are emotions? List as many as you can.
- Can you control your emotions, or do your emotions control you?
- Have you ever done something you regretted because of strong emotions? What else could you have done?
- How important is trust to a relationship?
- How do you develop trust? How do you destroy it?
- Is it ever okay to lie? If so, when?
- Is there anyone who would never lie to you? How do you feel about that person?
- How important is your attitude?
- Is attitude a choice?
- What would life be like if you always had a negative attitude?
- Do you know someone who is frequently angry or in a bad mood? Do you like being around them when they are that way?
- Do you consider yourself a good listener? How could you improve your listening skills?
- How do you know when someone is listening to you?
- What are some of humankind's greatest accomplishments? Were they accomplished by one person alone or with others?

**Educational and Diagnostic Meetings.** These types of meetings help teachers to discover student's prior knowledge of a particular subject and to informally assess student's learning. At the same time, they help students engage in higher-level thinking skills and make connections between curriculum and real life. Educational and diagnostic meetings might be held at almost any time:

- Before a lesson or unit of study to engage students' curiosity about the subject matter.
- In the middle of a unit of study to help the teacher assess how well the students are "getting it," so the teacher can determine whether to reteach certain content.
- During a unit to engage the students in critical-thinking skills regarding the content.
- At the end of the unit, to help review the learning and help the teacher determine if the students are ready for an assessment.
- After the assessment to help students extend their knowledge about that unit and prepare them for the next.

Because class-building meetings and educational and diagnostic meetings both deal with discovery, they can be conducted in a similar way (see Figure 3.9).

**Problem-Solving Meetings.** Even in the most effectively managed classroom, class problems occasionally occur. These occasions are excellent opportunities for students to be involved in real-life problem solving. The class meeting format can be helpful in addressing the class problem. The following situations might call for a problem-solving meeting:

- The students want more time to work on an assigned project.
- There have been too many instances of put-downs in the classroom.
- The students want to raise money for a field trip.
- The teacher and students want to develop a fair system for using the classroom computers.

Although many situations lend themselves to the class meeting approach to problem solving, there are still many that are meant for the teacher to resolve: behavior problems involving an individual, conflicts between two students, incidents of cheating, or blatant violations of school rules. Use your judgment (see Figure 3.10). One thing that worked well for me was to have a Class Meetings Suggestion Box where students could deposit suggestions about topics that they thought a

---

FIGURE 3.9

## Suggested Format for Class-Building Meetings and Educational and Diagnostic Meetings

### Define, Personalize, Challenge

1. *DEFINE* the topic, concept, or problem

   *Examples:*
   - Social Studies: What are the characteristics of a good leader?
   - English: What does the word *conflict* mean?
   - Math: What does the term *probability* mean?
   - Science: What does *energy* mean?
   - Health: What does *wellness* mean?

2. *PERSONALIZE* the topic, concept, or problem

   *Examples:*
   - Social Studies: Have you known a good (bad) leader?
   - English: Have you ever been involved in any kind of conflict?
   - Math: Have you ever taken a chance (bet on anything, flipped a coin, played "Rock, Paper, Scissors")?
   - Science: What are some types of energy you use every day?
   - Health: What do you do to maintain your overall wellness?

3. *CHALLENGE* the group's thinking

   *Examples:*
   - Social Studies: Was _____ a good leader? Why or why not?
   - English: Can all conflicts be resolved? Give examples.
   - Math: When in your life will it be useful for you to determine the probability of something?
   - Science: Are all the ways we generate electrical energy equal? Are some better than others? Why?
   - Health: What are some ways you could achieve a higher degree of overall wellness?

*Source:* Created by Al Katz

class meeting could address. I would then screen the requests, talk to individual students if necessary, and determine whether a class meeting was the appropriate way to address the issue. Some students love class meetings so much, they'll try to find ways to have them every day.

Another important consideration in holding a problem-solving meeting is to make sure the students know up front how much decision-making power they will have regarding any particular issue:

- Do you just want their input, but the final decision will be yours?

- Are you an equal member of the classroom community, and your opinion carries the same weight as any other member?

- Are you delegating the decision to the class, and anything they decide is what you will support?

Depending on the issue and the age and maturity of your students, you will need to use your judgment regarding the appropriate level of

---

FIGURE 3.10

## Suggested Format for Problem-Solving Meetings

1. State the problem and define any terms.
2. Describe the desired state, asking, "What do we want? or, "How do we want it to be?"
3. Describe the present state, asking, "How is it now?"
4. Examine current behavior, asking, "What are we currently doing re-garding _____?" or, "What have we been doing in regard to _____?"
5. Evaluate the current behavior, asking, "Is what we are currently doing getting us what we want?" (If the answer is yes, you may be done. If the answer is no, continue.)
6. Brainstorm possible plans, asking, "What else might we try to get us what we want?"
7. Make a plan. Have students rate the proposed plans on a scale of 1–10 and choose the plan that seems most likely to succeed.

*Source:* Adapted from William Glasser's Reality Therapy.

decision-making power you will invest in them. To avoid misunder-standing, it is best to simply state the level of decision-making power to them at the very beginning of the problem-solving meeting. If students believe they have more decision-making power than they really do, your relationship with them could be seriously damaged. If the students are empowered to make the decision, one other consideration is how the final decision will be made—by majority rule or consensus?

Although teachers have much to consider before using a problem-solving class meeting, they also should consider the great benefits to the students. They will be using their verbal and critical-thinking skills in real situations while experiencing the power of democratic principles.

## Conclusions

Humans are social creatures: We are born with genetic instructions to form and maintain relationships, and to gain a sense of belonging in whatever circumstances we find ourselves in. Just as it is difficult to focus on work or learning when we are extremely hungry or cold, it is difficult to work or learn when we feel alone and isolated.

Getting students out of isolation and into community helps create an optimum learning environment. Schools provide warmth, shelter, and food for students, knowing that without these essentials, students cannot learn well. If we also intentionally feed the need to belong and feel accepted, we will increase the likelihood of quality learning and responsible behavior.

4

# Power in the Classroom: Creating the Environment

IN HIS 1962 ADDRESS AT THE UNIVERSITY OF CALIFORNIA AT BERKELEY, PRESIDENT John F. Kennedy stated, "In this time of turbulence and change, it is more true than ever that knowledge is power." Most would agree that, as we begin the 21st century, we are again in a time of turbulence, and change is happening at an ever-increasing pace. Because the purpose of education is to provide children with the knowledge and skills—in other words, the power—to live healthy, successful lives, power should be the need that schools most effectively address. Ironically, power is the need that many students find most difficult to meet in school. In *The Quality School*, Glasser relates what he has discovered from interviewing students throughout the United States about their school experience:

> When I present my ideas to teachers and administrators, I usually inter-
> view six junior or senior high school students in front of a large
> audience. Because for young people the need for power is very difficult
> to satisfy, I always ask, "Where in school do you feel important?" This
> question always seems to the students to come from outer space; they
> look at me as if I had asked something ridiculous . . . . However, if I
> persist, most students tell me that they feel important in their extracur-
> ricular activities: Sports, music, and drama are frequently mentioned.
> Almost never mentioned are academic classes. (1992, p. 47)

In academic classes, students are told how to behave, what to learn, when and how to learn it, and then are assessed in ways that may not take into account the diverse intelligences that exist in every student population. Often when students ask, "Why do we have to learn this?", they are treated to a cold stare or told, "Because it's on the test." Then, if the students are unsuccessful in proving that they learned what has been demanded of them in the way that the system has decided they must prove it, they are punished with low grades. Worse, the system labels them "failures." In this kind of system, students are powerless.

I'm not suggesting that we do away with carefully crafted curricula or let the students "take over" the classroom. Coaches, music teachers, and drama teachers don't let the students tell them how to do their jobs, yet students feel empowered and important in sports, band, chorus, and in school plays, often work harder at these pursuits than they do in academic classes, and generally achieve higher-quality results. What I am suggesting is that teachers can employ a number of strategies that help students gain power in school.

An important concept for teachers to understand is that by helping to empower students, teachers enjoy more, not less, power. Remember the way Choice Theory defines *power*. First, there is *power over*, which is frequently the first thing that comes to mind when we hear the word *power*. This is the urge to control others, maybe for personal satisfaction, maybe "for their own good." Second, there is *power within*. This might be called personal empowerment, which includes learning, accomplishing goals, and achieving competence or excellence. Third is *power with*, which is the power we achieve when we work cooperatively with others. Traveling to the moon and back would be an example of the power that can be harnessed when people work together. Every day in school, students can meet their need for power if teachers and others provide them with opportunities to achieve *power with* and *power within*. If students do not have opportunities to meet their need for power in these healthy, productive, and responsible ways, they will most likely choose *power over*. Seeking *power over* might manifest itself in behaviors like cheating, bullying other students, disrupting a classroom, or engaging in vandalism or violence. Remember, we have choices about almost everything we do, but we do not have choices about experiencing powerful urges to meet our five basic needs.

Many teachers in my workshops complain about students who engage them in "power struggles." When teachers provide a number of opportunities for students to gain power, these students will work harder on their assignments, and behavioral problems will be reduced significantly, if not completely eliminated. This chapter explains dozens of specific strategies that teachers can use to provide students with responsible ways to meet their need for power by (1) giving students a say in the classroom, (2) helping students gain recognition, and (3) adopting other classroom procedures designed to help students gain personal empowerment in school. Chapter 5 then discusses empowerment strategies that help increase student success and achievement.

## Giving Students a Say in the Classroom

### The Class Constitution

One of the most effective and practical ways teachers can give students a say in the classroom is by allowing them to participate in developing the classroom rules or behavioral guidelines. Traditionally, rules are determined by the teacher and briefly explained on the first day of class. The teacher might say, "I've got two rules. Rule number one: Respect me, respect others, and respect yourself. Rule number two: Do your work. Any questions? Good." One benefit of this method of determining class rules is its efficiency; it takes less than two minutes. Another benefit is that these rules are simple and few.

The shortcomings of this method, however, outweigh the benefits. First, the expectations are vague. What does respecting the teacher look and sound like? How about respecting others or oneself? What does "Do your work" mean? Just do it, or do it well? If I do it, but don't bring it to class, is that okay? Second, the students have no ownership of the rules. While the teacher is explaining her expectations, some students are thinking, "Yeah, yeah, yeah. Here we go again," or are simply hearing what we hear on *Peanuts* cartoons when adults talk to Charlie Brown and his friends: "Wa wa waa wa waaaa." Unless the students understand specifically what is expected of them and how the expectations benefit them, there is little chance they will be motivated to meet those expectations. When a student breaks the rules in a situation like this, which is inevitable, the teacher will likely think that unless that student is punished, chaos will ensue. Punishment will result in resentment and rebellion, creating an adversarial teacher-student relationship, and a cycle of discipline problems commences that ends only when summer vacation begins. A classroom like this is no fun for either the students or the teacher, and very little, if any, quality work is accomplished.

If the teacher engages the students in developing clear behavioral guidelines that the students see as adding quality to their school lives, the relationship between the students and the teacher is enhanced. What's more, students will be much less likely to disrupt the learning environment, which in turn increases the likelihood that students will achieve quality work. As Sullo states in *Inspiring Quality in Your School*, "If there were ever to be a revolution in the United States, it would probably not begin in Congress" (1997, p. 98). In other words, people who make the rules are less likely to break them. There are many ways to engage students in developing the class rules. The following process is a way I've found to be effective with students of all ages. The process not only allows the students to be a part of creating a shared vision of a quality classroom, helping them meet their need for power and instilling a sense of responsibility for their learning environment, it's also fun:

- *Step 1: Identify the Behaviors and Attitudes.* Ask each student to write down the way she would like to be treated in school. What behaviors and attitudes would she see and hear? Also, what behaviors and attitudes would she *not* see or hear? Next, this student joins with two or three other students, and the group comes up with a list they can all agree on.

- *Step 2: Create a Living Space.* Provide each small group with a large piece of chart paper or newsprint, and ask each group to draw a living space. A living space is anywhere people can be: an island, a boat, a hot air balloon, a village, a house, and so on.

- *Step 3: Create Symbols.* Direct each group of students to create a picture symbol representing each of the behaviors they identified as a group. For example, if they identified put-downs as a behavior they did not want to see or hear, they might use a picture of a hand performing a "thumbs down" gesture. If they identified support as a behavior they did want, they might use a picture of a bridge to represent support.

- *Step 4: Placing the Symbols in the Living Space.* Direct the students to draw the symbols of the behaviors they do want to see and hear in their classroom *inside* the living space and to draw the symbols of the behaviors they do not want to see or hear *outside* the living space. To ensure clarity, the students may want to label the symbols. Remember, the quality of the drawing is not as important as engaging everyone in the group in the process of its creation.

- *Step 5: Group Presentations.* Have each group present its final product to the class. Have a student keep a list of all the behaviors and attitudes that the groups address. This list will help in the next step.

- *Step 6: The Whole Class Living Space.* After each small group has presented its drawing, engage the whole class in a discussion to come to consensus on the behaviors that all the students *would* like and *not* like to have in the classroom. Create another living space, and engage all the students in drawing of the symbols.

At this point, you can take the opportunity to examine the underlying principles or values that form the foundation for specific behaviors listed by the class. Those will most likely include, among others, the five universal ethical principles of respect, responsibility, caring, fairness, and honesty. You will most likely need to guide the students as they identify these foundational principles, asking questions such as, "If we want to avoid put-downs in our classroom, what do we value?"

You may want to write the guiding principles underneath your living space, literally creating its foundation. If you don't think the students have identified all the behaviors you'd like them to, you can use these foundational principles to help them. You could ask, "What does fairness look like or sound like in the classroom?" This way, you'll be sure to have a clear, complete constitution. If students still have not identified a behavior that you feel strongly about, add it to the list, explaining that you are a member of the class community and, therefore, have a right to have your input as well.

- *Step 7: Give to Get.* After the students have articulated a vision of the way they would like to see their classroom, ask them what they will have to be willing to give in order to achieve that goal. Students will understand the concept that to be treated in a certain way, they must treat others that way.

- *Step 8: Get a Commitment.* This step is critical if the constitution is to succeed. Get a commitment from each student to do his best to live up to the behavioral guidelines listed. A verbal commitment is good, but a written commitment is better. Many teachers who use this strategy ask each student to sign the final document. Next, the document is laminated, goes on the wall, and becomes the class constitution for behavior throughout the year.

- *Step 9: Keep It Alive.* The process of developing the class constitution helps build class involvement and ownership of the rules, but that alone is not enough to keep the document alive. Frequently referring to the document, especially for the first few weeks, is critical to its success. When class has gone well, stop and ask, "Are we keeping to our constitution? How's it working for us? What can we each do to keep it alive?" It is important to refer to it not only when there are problems, or all references to the constitution will likely be perceived in a negative way. Many students will think, "Oh, no! Now we're in trouble!" anytime the teacher refers to it. If, however, it is referred to when things are going well and when there are difficulties, it is seen more as what it truly is, a shared picture of the way the classroom should be. The constitution then becomes an important part of the class culture.

Beginning the year or the semester by developing a class constitution empowers students in a way few other strategies can. It shows the class members that the teacher trusts them to be responsible for their behavior and for their own learning. This is a strategy that has been very successful for me not only as a classroom teacher, but also as a coach, a play director, and a club advisor. Any time people are working together toward a common goal, developing a shared vision of how they hope to work together builds a sense of teamwork and helps prevent conflict.

## Classroom Needs Circle

Another way to provide students with an opportunity to have a say in the classroom is to develop a Classroom Needs Circle. This strategy is one I learned from Becky Sue Bianco, a middle school reading teacher in Watkins Glen, New York. Using this strategy, the teacher begins the year teaching her students about the basic human needs. After the students have gained an understanding of the genetic instructions that drive our behavior, the teacher explains the difference between responsible and irresponsible behavior, using Glasser's definition. Responsible behavior is that which enables us to meet our needs without making it more difficult for others to meet theirs. The students, working in pairs or small groups, list specific behaviors that would enable them to meet each of their psychological needs (love and belonging, power, freedom, and fun) in responsible ways in the classroom. Next, the teacher leads a whole-class discussion, coming to consensus on a list of behaviors derived from those developed in the pairs or small groups. After consensus, the teacher writes the behaviors agreed upon in the appropriate quadrants of a circle like the one in Figure 4.1.

Once the Classroom Needs Circle is completed to the satisfaction of the students and the teacher, it is posted on the wall. Like the Classroom Constitution, the students and teacher should refer to it frequently and use it to help themselves evaluate their behavior. Both the Class Constitution and the Classroom Needs Circle should be thought of as living documents, which can be amended at any time in an ongoing effort to attain a match between the teacher's and students' mental pictures of a quality classroom and reality.

## Student-Generated Curriculum

This strategy for empowering students may not work in every subject area or at every grade level because of the amount of state or district control over the course content. In many classrooms, however, teachers can boost student motivation by engaging them in the process of curriculum development.

**Student-Chosen Themes.** Doug Stevens, a 7th grade English teacher in Cincinnati, explains to his students, "This year we are in this classroom to improve the way we listen, speak, read, and write." He

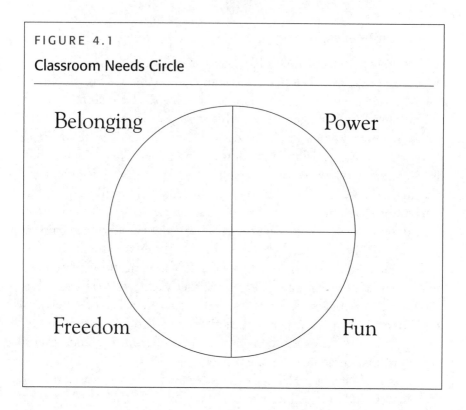

FIGURE 4.1

Classroom Needs Circle

Belonging    Power

Freedom    Fun

reads his students the state standards for each communication strand, and then asks them, "What do you want to listen, speak, read, and write *about?*" If you were to adopt Doug's strategy, at this point you might lead the class in brainstorming a mind map of all the topics that you could choose from. Then you might give each student five votes that he could distribute any way he'd like, using them all for one topic or spreading them around to five different topics. Finally, you might pick the top three or four topics for your content for the year, through which you can teach the skills the students need to fulfill district or state English language arts requirements.

**Know-Want-Learned (KWL).** This is a well-known strategy for beginning a new unit of study. Students are first asked what they *know* about a particular topic. This helps the teacher determine how much prior knowledge students have about the subject they're about to study, helping her connect new information into what they already know. The *W* represents the question, "What do you *want* to know about this topic?" Pursuing some of the topics generated by this question may take the class in directions that the teacher never planned on, but has the potential to lead the class into a highly motivated learning experience. At the end of the unit, the teacher helps the students articulate all that they have *learned* through this collaborative approach to the curriculum.

## Giving Students Recognition

One of the synonyms for power as Glasser defines it is "recognition." It feels good when we achieve something; it also feels good when others recognize our achievements. I'd like to differentiate recognition from rewards and praise, however. After years of recommending the use of rewards as shapers of student behavior, many educators have come to recognize the negative impact of extrinsic rewards on students. As Kohn explains in *Punished by Rewards*, there are four negative outcomes associated with the use of praise. "First, when someone is praised for doing something that isn't very difficult, she may take this to mean she isn't very smart" (1993, p. 98). This may result in lower expectations for success at difficult tasks, hindering his ability to achieve good work later on. "Second, telling someone how good she is can increase the pressure she feels to live up to the compliment. This pressure, in turn, can make her more self-conscious, a state that often interferes with performance." Third, praise "encourages some children to become dependent on the evaluations offered by their teachers and those who are unable to meet their teachers' expectations . . . ultimately decide to give up trying . . . . Finally, praise, like other rewards, often undermines the intrinsic motivation that leads people to do their best" (p. 99).

For our purposes, I am going to define praise as positive comments, the purposes of which have to do more with what the praiser is trying to achieve than the person being praised. Statements such as "See how nicely Miguel is sitting" or "Great speech, Samantha!" are more manipulation than recognition; it is using praise to control. Recognition is not an attempt to control; it is highly specific and provides students with opportunities for learning or for celebrating their successes. The rest of this section will provide examples of ways of giving students recognition.

## Specific Feedback

Writing "Great Job" on the top of a paper may be expedient and feel good to the teacher, but it doesn't help the student learn. What made it a great job, so the student can do it again or do it better next time? "Excellent use of concrete, supporting details for your topic sentence" might help the young writer learn how to develop a paragraph. Or, "clear diction and appropriate volume" might help a student improve his presentation skills. It's important that we help students evaluate what they did well, as long as the information we provide is specific and accurate. "Feedback is one of the greatest sources of intrinsic motivation" (Jensen, 1998, p. 67). Feedback can be given in writing or as part of a one-on-one conversation between the teacher and a student.

## Parent Postcards

We often send notes or official interim reports to parents when there are academic or behavior difficulties. Sending a postcard home recognizing a student's achievements can have powerful positive results, strengthening your relationship with both the student and the parents, important factors in that student's continued success in school. It is a small investment of time that pays off.

## Celebrations

Say all of your students achieved mastery on a particular assessment. Why not have a pizza party! Some might ask, "But isn't that a reward?" No, it's a celebration. If you said to the students before the assessment, "If you achieve mastery, we'll have a pizza party!" then it would be a reward. In this case, you are not trying to manipulate anyone's behavior; you are simply expressing your delight in their success. If a student asks, "Hey, if we do well on the next project, can we have another pizza party?" you might say no and explain the difference between a bribe (or reward) and a celebration. Other ways of celebrating might have less extrinsic value than a pizza party. You might create some classroom ritual for celebrating success like a dance of joy, a "happy wiggle," creating a unique classroom handshake, or playing celebratory music such as "The Theme to Rocky" or Aaron Copland's "Fanfare for the Common Man."

## Peer Recognition

At the end of a unit or at the end of a week, month, or semester, have students give recognition to each other. One way to do this is to have the students write their name on an envelope and place a blank piece of paper in the envelope. Have the students sit in a circle and pass their envelopes to the person to their right. Each student takes the piece of paper out of the envelope and writes down a strength that they recognized in that student during the last unit, week, semester, or year. It is more effective if the students also write a specific time when they noticed each person's strength. For example, a student might write, "A strength that D.J. brought to this class this week was his creativity. He came up with a neat title for the skit we wrote in class." There are many variations on this activity. For example, you might have students pin 5" x 8" cards to one another's back, then go around the room, writing strengths on as many students backs as they can in 10 minutes. You might enjoy taking part in this activity yourself.

## Publish

A great way to celebrate students' success is to allow them to publish what they assess to be their best work. There are many ways students can publish their work. It's best when they help choose the work they believe is worth publishing. Some of the ways you and the students can publish their work are to

- Create a "Brag Board," a bulletin board where students put work they are proud of.
- Display work in the halls, the cafeteria, or the library.
- Hold a Young Authors' Night for students to read their work for parents and friends (or Young Historians' Night, Young Scientists' Night, Young Artists' Night, and so on).
- Create a booklet of student work.
- Send work to publications that specialize in publishing student work.
- Make class presentations.

## Classroom Strategies That Help Students Gain Power

Teachers can adopt other classroom procedures designed to help students gain personal empowerment in school.

### Listening to Students

One of the most effective ways to help people meet their need for power is simply to listen to them. It is not necessary that we agree with them, but it is essential that they believe they've been heard and understood. There are a few ways of listening to students in the classroom.

**Class Meetings.** The class meeting format is one of the most effective practices for allowing students to express their thoughts, feelings, and opinions and to be listened to by both the teacher and the other students. The class meeting format I recommend is explained in detail in Chapter 3.

**Journal Entries.** Reading and, most important, responding to students' journal entries is another effective way to help students feel like they are being listened to. You might engage students with journal prompts that invite them to

- Make suggestions about classroom policies and procedures.
- Express an opinion on global, national, local, or school events.
- Comment on or ask questions regarding the class content.
- Share something about themselves.

A brief, positive response in the margin lets the student know she has been heard and acknowledged.

**Suggestion Box.** Keep a suggestion box somewhere in the room and invite students to use it to express thoughts, concerns, and opinions regarding classroom policies and procedures or to communicate private messages to you.

**Kid of the Week.** At the Huntington Woods Elementary School in Wyoming, Michigan, the first Glasser Quality School, teachers and students observe "Kid of the Week." Each student's life is celebrated in the classroom for a full school week. At the beginning of the school year, each student is provided with a blank copy of a book entitled *All About Me*, and is given the assignment to complete the pages with photographs, drawings, stories, and lists of things such as "My Family," "My Friends," "Ways I Meet My Needs," and "Things I Like to Do." During each student's week, five to ten minutes of each day are dedicated to listening to the Kid of the Week share a page out of his book. On the last day of the week, the student teaches his class about something that he enjoys: coin collecting, making burritos, karate, and so forth. The finale of the celebration is the class singing a song in appreciation of that week's kid. Teachers I've worked with have discussed how they have used variations on Kid of the Week. Some have students create an "All About Me" T-shirt that is unique for each student. Others help each student develop an "All About Me" bulletin board.

**Needs Collage.** An activity I have found popular with students is the Needs (or Quality World) Collage. First, ask students to bring in as many magazines as possible from home. After the students have learned about the five basic human needs, they go through the magazines and cut out pictures and words that represent ways that they might meet each of their needs. Then they arrange and glue the pictures and words on poster board. It's great if you can laminate their final products. Over the next few days, part of each class can be set aside to have the students share their collages with the class. I've done this activity with students from 1st through 12th grade. They all completed their works of art with equal enthusiasm.

## Class Jobs

Students feel important when they are allowed to take responsibility for class jobs. As a child, I remember feeling really "cool" when it was my responsibility to take the attendance cards to the office. Clapping erasers was also a thrill. Any time you can give students responsibilities for necessary tasks, it is an opportunity for them to gain power. You might ask students to read the morning announcements, collect or distribute papers, or organize supplies. Different classrooms need different tasks. I'll leave it to you to decide which tasks you might delegate to your students.

 *Note:* Students will often surprise you with what they can do and how well they can do it.

## Peer Tutors

Employing students to teach or tutor other students empowers both the student doing the teaching and, by increasing her chances for success, the student being tutored. It can also help bridge the time gap between the students who achieve mastery on the first assessment and those who need more time. Simply telling the peer tutors to go help their fellow classmates is usually not enough. A child may be an excellent student, but not necessarily an excellent teacher. You might develop a training program for a few days after school to teach students how to help their classmates effectively and tactfully.

## Peer Mediators

Many schools have developed peer mediation programs, which teach students to resolve conflict between other students. Why not teach all of the students in the classroom these skills? Should conflicts arise in the classroom, depending on their severity, you might give the students involved the option of working it out themselves, working with a peer mediator whom you select, or involving you, the teacher, in resolving the problem. Students will often choose to work it out themselves or with a peer mediator. This helps students learn to be independent problem solvers, while enabling the teacher to accomplish other work. There are many conflict resolution models available. The one I recommend is Glasser's Structured Reality Therapy, which involves the idea of the Solving Circle, which he explains further in *Choice Theory* (1998).

## Teach and Tell

This activity is simply a variation of a favorite for many students in the primary grades: Show and Tell, a practice that encourages children to bring in from home something of importance to them and tell the rest of the class about it. Show and Tell provides students with a wonderful opportunity to meet their need for power. The whole class is listening as they teach their classmates something that no one in the class knows as much about as they do. Why stop this practice in 1st grade? In most states, English Language Arts (ELA) standards include something about speaking and listening for information and understanding. Why not expand Show and Tell into Teach and Tell and address the ELA standard while providing an opportunity for students to feel important and gain recognition for something they are proud of? This activity encourages students to tell the class about something they like or do well and teach the class how to do it. In teaching 12th grade English, I found my Teach and Tell unit to be among the students' favorites. They learned to make an organized, engaging oral presentation while developing effective speaking and listening skills. Behavior problems during Teach and Tell are virtually nonexistent because students know that the way they treat their peers will be the way their peers treat them when it's their turn.

Also, Teach and Tell is a great way to increase class connectedness as you and the rest of the class learn important things about one another's interests and skills. Some of the most memorable presentations my students made were How to Detail a Car, How to Make "African Egg Rolls," Motorcycle Maintenance, Archery Basics, Field Goal Kicking, Fencing, How to Play a Drum Roll, How to Apply Makeup, Comic Book Collecting, and How to Sell Newspaper Subscriptions Over the Telephone. Kids have a tremendous amount of nonacademic knowledge and many outside interests to share. Teach and Tell gives them an opportunity to be successful academically using something they love to do and do well.

## Seven Deadly Habits

Most of the strategies in this book are things teachers can do to help students meet their needs. But this strategy refers to seven behaviors teachers ought to avoid. Glasser refers to these common behaviors as the "Seven Deadly Habits": criticizing, blaming, complaining, nagging, threatening, punishing, and bribing. Not only do these behaviors destroy relationships, they widen the power gap that already exists between teachers and students (2000b).

I learned the destructive power of criticism in the classroom the hard way. After I first read Glasser's *The Quality School*, I started out the school year intentionally creating a needs-satisfying classroom environment. After a month or so, I was enthusiastic over how well all my classes were going. The students all seemed to genuinely enjoy the class, there were no behavior problems, and I believed that this would be the most successful year I'd ever had teaching. Then I collected the first major writing assignment of the year, took it home, and graded it the way I always had in the past—writing extensive comments in the margins about the mistakes and weaknesses I observed in their essays. I handed back their papers on the following Monday. Within minutes, the wonderful class climate I'd worked so hard to create was gone. Some students were glaring at me. Others would not make eye contact. Still others were muttering under their breath. I was so shocked, I didn't know what to do, so I tried to engage the class in cooperative group discussions about the reading we'd done the night before. All the groups talked about, though, was the paper they just got back. At first, I felt angry and defensive, thinking to myself, "What a bunch of babies! After all I've done to make this class fun and interesting, they can't take a little 'constructive criticism'?"

I wrote that day's class off and did some serious soul-searching at home that evening. What I realized was that all the class-building and needs-satisfying teaching strategies in the world could not prepare them for what they obviously perceived as criticism of their essays. The next day we had a class meeting about my role as an English teacher. At first, they were withdrawn, but when they realized that I was sincere in my effort to rebuild our relationship, they were more forthcoming. One student offered his opinion: "Well, I guess it is your job to point out our mistakes, but you could tell us a few things we did right!"

"Yeah," said another, "I worked a long time on this paper. I must have done something right."

"So, what you're telling me is if I tell you what you're doing right, you'll be okay with my telling you what's wrong?" I asked.

Another student answered, "Well, yeah, but on my paper you wrote 'Weak introduction!' What am I supposed to learn from that? How am I supposed to make it strong?"

By the end of the class meeting, the students agreed that it was my job to help them improve their writing by pointing out their weaknesses, and I agreed to also point out their strengths and to be as specific as possible in my comments. We all agreed that my remarks would be considered helpful feedback rather than criticism. The class atmosphere gradually returned to the way it was, and I learned to have that conversation with future classes before assigning the first essay.

Although Glasser considers criticism the deadliest of the Seven Deadly Habits, the others are not much better. Blaming and complaining may temporarily make the teacher feel in control, but they focus on the past, not on solving the present problem, and only serve to damage the relationship. The other four (nagging, threatening, punishing, and bribing) are all coercive techniques designed to make someone do what we want them to do. None of them teach self-discipline, responsibility, or independence, and all of them destroy the relationship that we need if we want to have any influence with students in the future. Instead of relying on the Seven Deadly Habits, Glasser recommends replacing them with what he calls the "Seven Caring Habits": caring, listening, supporting, contributing, encouraging, trusting, and befriending (2000b). These habits, especially listening, empower students while widening the teacher's sphere of influence.

## Students of Choice

This strategy, teaching students Choice Theory, is the last strategy in this chapter not because it's the least important, but because it may be the most. When students learn and start using the ideas of Choice Theory in their lives, everyone benefits. Students learn these ideas easily and readily because they can relate to them. Choice Theory is all about their lives. Some of the benefits of teaching this theory to students include the following:

- *Students gain an understanding of themselves.* Through learning about the Basic Human Needs and Quality World pictures, students learn what motivates them. Understanding these concepts helps them maintain a healthy balance in their lives. They learn, for example, that if they spend too much time trying to meet their needs for power and freedom, their needs for belonging or fun may suffer. A student's understanding of his personal needs profiles may help him gain a better understanding of his unique identity, in turn helping him make important life decisions such as what occupation best suits him.

- *Students gain an understanding of others.* Understanding the Basic Human Needs assists students in seeing our common humanity. This appreciation can help students learn tolerance of and compassion for others in our increasingly diverse society.

- *Students will learn they are responsible for their behavior.* Along with the fundamental assumption of Choice Theory that all of our behavior is chosen comes the corollary that we are responsible for the choices we make. This concept is one that can help students learn early on that they are the masters of their destiny. Frequently discussing behavior in these terms enables students to examine the effectiveness of the choices they make.

- *Students will have the resources to build and maintain relationships.* Understanding Choice Theory will decrease the likelihood that students will engage in coercive behaviors in their interactions with others. They may resort less often to the Seven Deadly Habits, turning more often to the Caring Habits, thus nurturing rather than destroying the important relationships in their lives.

- *Students will be able to develop productive habits of mind.* An understanding of the basic components of Choice Theory and the process of reality therapy gives students the potential to develop the skills that Daniel Goleman (1995) calls "emotional intelligence" and Robert Marzano (1997) calls the "productive habits of mind." These are skills such as restraining impulsivity, planning effectively, self-evaluating, delaying gratification, maintaining an open mind, persevering, monitoring one's thoughts, and managing stress.

- *Students and teachers will share a common language.* If you base your classroom management strategies on Choice Theory, students will gain a better understanding of your teaching and management styles if they learn it, too. Also, your students' understanding of Choice Theory can provide a framework for discussions involving motivation, differing perceptions, effective and responsible behavior, and many other topics that frequently come up in any classroom. It can simply improve communications between you and your students.

- *Choice Theory can easily relate to course content.* In language arts, Choice Theory provides students with a host of speaking and writing topics (for example, How I Meet My Basic Needs, Some of the Pictures in My Quality World, A Time My Scales Were Out of Balance, and How One of My Perceptions Has Changed). In literature or social studies classes, students can analyze literary characters, historical figures, or people in the news in terms of their internal motivation. After examining a character's total behavior, students can try to determine which need or needs seem to be the primary motivator behind the behavior. Or, students can analyze the quality world pictures driving a character's behavior and try to determine the underlying values the character seems to hold. This way of analyzing real or fictional characters helps make historical events or literary themes spring to life.

## Conclusions

Effective teachers understand that by providing students with many and varied ways of meeting their need for power, they are helping prevent behavioral problems. In other words, by appealing to students' need for *power within* and *power with*, the teacher is avoiding *power over* struggles. Contrary to a widely held belief, power is not a commodity, where one person loses power if another gains it. If we empower students by giving them a voice in the classroom and really listen to what they say, if we regularly provide all students with recognition for the unique strengths they bring to the class, and if we intentionally provide students with other ways of feeling like they make important contributions to the class, we are creating an empowering environment. By empowering students, teachers actually empower themselves.

5

# Power in the Classroom: Strategies for Student Achievement

ONE OF THE MOST EFFECTIVE WAYS TO HELP STUDENTS MEET THEIR NEED FOR power in the classroom is to help them experience success through producing competent, or even better quality, work. When students do not feel successful in the academic classroom, generally two things happen. First, they give up on academics as a way of achieving success, and second, they look to other activities to meet the need for personal empowerment. Some students are successful in meeting their need for power through extracurricular activities such as sports, music, art, and drama. Those that are not successful may find that disrupting the learning environment for everyone else gives them a sense of power, saying, in effect, "I'd rather be 'bad' than a failure." While some students simply drop out, still others engage in even more potentially harmful activities: gang membership, drug and alcohol abuse, violence, or sex. Conversely, when students feel successful in school, they are more likely to replicate that success and less likely to disrupt the learning environment or engage in self-destructive behaviors.

Literally hundreds of books have been written on how to increase learning and achievement. I won't attempt to list every effective strategy known to boost student achievement, but I will discuss a number of effective strategies consistent with Choice Theory. These strategies fall under the four general headings of curriculum, instruction, assessment, and miscellaneous classroom strategies.

## Curriculum

"Why do we have to learn this?" is a question asked by students of all ages in classrooms all over the United States. It deserves a reasonable response. Unfortunately, in many classrooms the answer is "Because I said so," "Because it's on the test," or "Because if you don't, you will fail." What the students are asking is, "How is what you are asking me to learn going to add quality to my life?" If we can't answer that question about a particular lesson or unit, maybe we shouldn't be teaching it. In *Every Student Can Succeed* (2000b), Glasser differentiates education from a practice he calls "schooling." Education is not simply acquiring knowledge, which is a definition that educators have used for centuries. It is, instead, using knowledge and gaining skills that can improve the quality of our lives, a definition that is congruent with the information age we live in. *Schooling*, on the other hand, is "an education-destroying practice that requires students . . . to spend fifty to eighty percent of their time acquiring skills and memorizing knowledge they will rarely use outside of school" (p. 66).

*Schooling* includes practices such as requiring students to memorize state capitals, the number of sonnets Shakespeare wrote, the Dewey Decimal System, the value of *pi* to five decimals, the Periodic Table of the Elements, and so on. These are bits of information that successful, productive members of society do not need on a daily basis, and which can be looked up if they are needed. (Now there's a useful skill: learning how to find information.) I'm not saying all memorization is a bad thing. Most people would agree that knowing the multiplication tables, for example, is extremely useful. A question that teachers ought to ask before requiring students to memorize something is, "Is this information essential to a person's success in the real world?"

If teachers eliminate schooling from their curriculum, they'll be free to educate students, teaching them skills they will need to be successful in their personal and professional lives. Most teachers, students, parents, and leaders of business and industry agree on the skills that are required for success in the real world. These skills include

- Communicating: reading, writing, listening, and speaking;
- Reasoning: comparing, classifying, using inductive and deductive reasoning, and analyzing;
- Problem solving: investigating, decision making, and experimenting;
- Critical thinking;
- Creative thinking;
- Self-regulated thinking;
- Leading; and
- Working cooperatively.

Focusing on teaching these real-world skills and eliminating the teaching of relatively useless information helps students gain the skills that they'll need in the 21st century, enabling the teacher to answer the age-old question, "Why do we have to learn this?"

Unfortunately, some of the curricula that would fall under the "schooling" definition are dictated by school districts or by the state. If you are in a situation where some schooling is mandated, rather than eliminate it, simply try to minimize it. Fortunately, as more states attempt to raise educational standards, they are implementing new assessments that actually test the higher-level skills previously listed. As districts realign their curricula with the new assessments, teachers involved in curriculum development have an excellent opportunity to emphasize education and eliminate schooling. Rather than waiting for the inevitable "Why do we have to learn this?", a more proactive approach would be to start each unit or lesson by explaining to the students the knowledge and skills they'll be learning during the unit and their importance in the real world. Even better, engage the students in a discussion of how those skills might benefit them in the future. Some teachers bring in speakers from the community (parents, school board members, business leaders) to discuss the importance of these skills in the business or professional world. When students see that what they are being asked to learn will benefit them in the short or long term, they are much more likely to become engaged in the learning and perform competently.

## Instruction

Offering a useful curriculum is one important way to help students meet their need for personal power in school, enabling them to see that school will empower them to succeed when they are on their own. However, even the most compelling curriculum will fail to increase student achievement unless the instructional strategies are well designed. Children live in the now. They are interested in how the knowledge and skills we're asking them to learn are going to help them in the long term, but they are more interested in the answers to the questions: "Can I be successful at this?" and "What's in this for me today?" Varied and engaging instructional strategies are the answer to that question. Appealing to each student's primary learning style helps him believe he can be successful, and engaging students in a variety of learning experiences makes learning fun.

Most teachers already understand that they should appeal to visual, auditory, and tactile kinesthetic learning modes. When students who are kinesthetic learners are taught exclusively in ways that are visual or auditory, learning (gaining power) is more difficult. They see themselves as "dumb," which not only affects their self-esteem, but also increases the chances of behavior problems. Such problems in turn affect the learning of the whole class. In my classroom, I began each year by administering a series of tests to my students to help me understand them as workers and learners. I administered work style surveys, temperament sorters, and learning-style inventories. Through the latter, I found that the majority of the students who labeled themselves as poor students were kinesthetic learners. I then found that when I varied my instruction to include kinesthetic learning activities as well as auditory and visual ones, all students were more successful and more motivated to be there. Although most teachers understand the importance of providing differentiated instruction, many lack the specific strategies to do so. Some of the best ways of appealing to the various learning modes and engaging students as they learn come from brain-compatible learning strategists.

The Center for Accelerated Learning, an organization that special-izes in applying brain research to learning, has developed a practical approach to lesson design called SAVI (Meier, 1999). Using SAVI learning strategies, teachers can optimize learning. The acronym SAVI stands for:

| | |
|---|---|
| *S*omatic | Learning by doing. |
| *A*uditory | Learning by talking and listening. |
| *V*isual | Learning by observing. |
| *I*ntellectual | Learning by thinking. |

By intentionally including SAVI teaching and learning strategies in every lesson, or at least in every unit, teachers significantly increase the chances of their students' success. In this chapter, I've used the concept of SAVI to organize dozens of learning strategies compiled from several sources, including Eric Jensen's *Brain Compatible Strategies*, ASCD and McREL's (Mid-continent Regional Educational Laboratory), Dimen-sions of Learning program, and the Center For Accelerated Learning's *Course Builder* toolkit. Many of the strategies described fit under more than one SAVI learning category, but I've listed them under the cate-gory that seems predominant.

## Somatic

"Somatic is from the Greek word for body. It denotes tactile, kines-thetic, hands-on learning. Everyone learns better if they get physical while they learn. If their bodies don't move, their brains don't groove" (Meier, 1999). Optimal learning takes place when teachers alternate between passive teaching strategies, where students are sitting and lis-tening or watching, and active strategies, where students are moving about or manipulating things. Some somatic teaching-learning strate-gies are discussed in the following section.

**Cross-Lateral Exercises.** A great time to use cross-lateral exercises is before a new learning or when students are getting tired. These exer-cises require the left and right brain hemispheres to interact with each other, leading to better thinking and better learning. Have students stand, take a deep breath, reach up and pat themselves on the back, first with their right hands, then with their left. Another exercise is to have the students stand, reach behind themselves and alternately touch their hands to their opposite heels. Any activity where students cross their arms or legs over the body's center line from one side to another is a cross-lateral exercise (Jensen, 1997).

**Hot Potato Pretest.** Write pretest questions about the upcoming unit or lesson on 3" x 5" cards, one question per card. Give each student a card and have the class stand in a circle. Toss a soft rubber ball to one student and tell this person to read his question aloud to the group and then throw the ball to another student. The next student must either answer the question or toss the ball to another student. If a question can't be answered in three to five throws, collect the card and make sure your unit or lesson addresses that content piece. Continue until all questions have been addressed (Meier, 1999).

**Walking Class.** "Take your group for a walk outside if weather permits, and continue to teach as you walk. Trigger ideas related to the walk. For example, use shapes of the buildings to talk about mathematics, the style of architecture to talk about history . . . " (Jensen, 1997, p. 7). You might also talk about topics like habitat or adaptation based on what you see around you. When I taught 7th grade English, I would take my classes on a walk each fall to give students an experience to write a descriptive essay about. As we walked, I'd ask questions: "What do you smell? What do you see? Hear? Feel? How might you describe those things?"

**Walking Pair-Share.** After a minilecture on a chunk of content, pair students up and have them take a walk and discuss what they've just learned.

**Skits.** After a passive learning activity, have the students act out the information, system, process, or skill they just learned. They can play inanimate objects or abstract concepts as well as people, animals, and others. My high school psychology students found lectures and note-taking incredibly dull, but when combined with skits, they were engaged and energized. For example, one skit they performed demonstrated the way information is transmitted in the brain from one neuron to another, with students playing the parts of the neuron, the neurotransmitter, the synapse, and so on. With a little creativity, almost any information, skill, or process can be acted out. (See Formations in Chapter 3.)

**Model Building.** Ask students to create a model of the events, concepts, skills, or processes they are being asked to learn. You can provide students with construction paper, modeling clay, Legos, Tinkertoys, and other miscellaneous objects. Let them construct models representing various aspects of the course material and then ask them to describe their creations to the class (Meier, 1999).

**Question-and-Answer Shuffle.** Write questions about the content you've taught on one set of cards, the answers on another, and shuffle them. Next, pair students at desks or tables and tell them to match the questions with the answers.

**Walk Through the Steps.** Create large footprint or shoe shapes out of poster board. Write one step of a process or procedure on each footprint and lay them out on the floor in order. Then ask pairs of learners to walk through the steps, explaining the steps to each other as they go. A variation of this is to scramble the steps and have partners or teams rearrange them in the right sequence (Meier, 1999).

**Frisbee Review.** Students stand in a large circle. Whoever catches the Frisbee (or other object) says one thing they learned during the lesson or unit (Jensen, 1997).

**Puzzle Assembly.** Prepare for this activity by copying pictures of system components or content segments onto poster board. Cut the pictures into irregular shapes, and put them in an envelope. Give each pair or team of students a different puzzle and tell them to assemble it, discussing the system or content and how the various pieces relate to each other. Have students generate questions as they do this. Some examples: English teachers might have students assemble segments that represent the writing process; health or biology teachers might have students assemble the reproductive system; social studies students might construct a puzzle representing the three branches of government and their components; a technology teacher might have students construct a model of an internal combustion engine (Meier, 1999).

**In-Class Scavenger Hunt.** Prepare a list of questions about the topic. Write the answers on separate colored index cards, one answer per card. Then hide the cards around the room. Give learners the questions and tell them that the answers are hidden throughout the room. Encourage learners to work together to find the answers.

Afterward, go over the questions as a class, asking each learner to give at least one answer (Meier, 1999).

**Balloons Pop Quiz.** Write questions about course content on small slips of paper. Put these questions in balloons (one slip per balloon) and blow the balloons up. Make enough for each member of the class to have one. Then put the balloons in a big box or a garbage bag. At the beginning of class, dump the balloons out into the room and ask each student to pick one, telling them that they will find a surprise inside when they pop their balloon. Give them some time to research and answer the question. Tell them that they may use any person or resource in the room to answer the question. When time is up, ask each learner to read her question and give the answer to the class.

 *Caution:* You may want to warn your neighbors about this activity before you use Balloons Pop Quiz.

## Auditory

"Our auditory minds are stronger than we realize. Before Gutenberg invented the printing press, most information was passed from generation to generation by the oral tradition, including the great epics and myths of all ancient cultures. And hearing the great stories was not a monotone, coldly academic exercise, but a sonically rich experience involving the emotions and accompanied in some cases by rhythm and music. All learners learn by sounds, by dialogue, by reading out loud, by describing to someone what they just experienced or what they just heard, by talking to themselves, by remembering jingles and rhymes, and by repeating sounds in their heads" (Meier, 1999, p. 66).

When teachers think of appealing to students' auditory learning mode, lecture is the strategy that immediately comes to mind. Although lecture still has its place in a quality classroom, some alternative strategies are offered.

**Music as Inspiration.** According to Jensen (1997), brain research tells us two things about music and the brain. First, music has the power to energize the brain, preparing us for a new learning experience. Second, certain kinds of music can boost our intelligence. Listening to

Mozart's *Piano Sonata in D Major* has helped learners raise their intelligence scores on spatial-temporal reasoning after just 10 minutes of listening. The effect doesn't last, but can be reactivated at any time. Here are some of Jensen's recommendations from *Brain Compatible Strategies*:

- Play positive energizing music before the start of class (or during transitions between topics). You might use movie themes.
- Play specific compositions in moments of emotional highs (*Theme to Rocky*, Olympics music, *Hallelujah Chorus*, or trumpet fanfares).
- Play low-volume background baroque music to soothe, calm, and relax (Handel's *Water Music*, Vivaldi's *Four Seasons*, Bach's *Brandenburg Concertos*).

**Concert Preview.** Before starting a unit, place all the transparencies or flip chart pages that you plan to use in the unit in order. Play relaxing music and turn the lights down low. Explain to the learners that they are going to see a preview of the unit or lesson. Ask them to just silently watch the screen or flip chart, making notes if they want. Play the music and present your material slowly enough for them to see and read, but not copy. When finished, ask learners what they already knew and what sparked their curiosity, and discuss the major content areas to be covered (Meier, 1999).

 *Note:* After the lesson or unit and before the test, do a Concert Review to help learners generate any questions that they may still have about the course content.

**Audio Clips.** Create an audio clip that contains material you want to explain. The tape can contain

- A skit or hypothetical scenario;
- Course content accompanied by soothing music;
- A case study;
- An interview with a person explaining how he has used the course content; or
- An overview of the material you've covered or will be covering.

After playing the audio clip, divide the class into pairs or small groups and have students discuss what they've just heard. A recorder in each group might write down a list of questions or the most important points from the audio clip. After the small-group discussion, hold a whole-class discussion, sharing what was discussed in groups (Meier, 1999).

**Storytelling.** Develop a story that relates to the course material, making sure the points you want to emphasize are told in an engaging, attention-grabbing way. Before you begin telling your story, set the mood with appropriate background music. After the story, have pairs or groups of students discuss what they've heard, digging as much meaning out of it as possible. Afterward, you might have a designated reporter from each group report to the class what they gleaned from the story, and then lead a whole-class discussion (Meier, 1999).

**Mnemonics.** A mnemonic is a word, phrase, rhyme, or other device that provides a cue for information we want to remember. "Lefty loosy, righty tighty" helps us remember which way to turn a screw or nut. I've used "Thirty days has September . . . " hundreds of times. "Roy G. Biv" has helped generations remember the order of colors in the spectrum. You can create your own mnemonics to help students remember information or a process. Better yet, students can be taught to create their own rhymes, acronyms, or other mnemonic devices.

**Songs.** One of the most powerful memory aids is the song. How much longer would it have taken most of us to learn the alphabet if it weren't for "Now I Know My ABCs"? (I think some of us still secretly rely on it.) I've often heard frustrated teachers remark that some students can't remember a single thing about their course content, but know every word to popular songs or raps. There are, of course, a number of reasons for this phenomenon, but one important factor is that the lyrics they so readily learn are set to music or rhythm. Take the content you believe is important for learners to acquire and set it to a melody that everyone knows, or create a simple rap integrating the information or process you are trying to teach. You might consider buying a rhyming dictionary to help speed up the writing process.

**Guided Imagery.** Prepare a script to read to learners that guides them through a skill, a process, a system, or an experience they are learning about. Play some relaxing background music and ask the students to relax and close their eyes. Ask them to imagine vividly seeing, hearing, feeling, smelling, and tasting everything they are about to hear. Then read the script slowly, asking them to visualize themselves performing the skill, process, or procedure or simply to experience the event as you go. When the reading is over, ask the learners to turn to a partner and discuss what they just learned through the guided imagery experience. Ask them to identify any areas where they had trouble (Meier, 1999).

**Sense Imagery.** This strategy, which is not only auditory but involves all five senses, is based on a well-accepted principle that if students have the ability to create detailed mental images of information they are receiving, they can improve their comprehension and retention of the information. Further, according to Dimensions of Learning creator author Robert J. Marzano:

> The more senses [students] use to create those images, the better the results. These images can make a distant historical example seem more real and transform an abstraction that is difficult to understand into something more concrete. To help students cultivate this skill, when they are reading a book, viewing a film, listening to a discussion or lecture, or observing a demonstration, encourage them to use all five senses (Marzano & Pickering, 1997, p. 53).

Ask students to imagine and describe, either orally or in writing, what the information would look like, feel like, smell like, taste like, or sound like. This could be used for helping students imagine a scientific experiment, a physical exercise, a historical or current event, a foreign country, or a fictional incident. When teaching *Macbeth*, for example, I would ask the students to imagine the sensory experiences they might have in a medieval castle. After students wrote in their journals about the sights, sounds, smells, and feelings they might have experienced in a medieval castle, we would brainstorm lists of ideas on flip chart paper. Think of the ways you could use this strategy in your subject area or classroom.

## Visual

"Visual acuity is strong in everyone" (Meier, 1999). Although it is stronger in some people than in others, humans are visual creatures, with more of our brains devoted to visual processing than any other sense. According to Jensen, "The human brain can normally register over 36,000 images per hour. The eyes are designed to take in 30 million bits of information per second" (1998). This section is devoted to helping you take advantage of this physiological phenomenon.

**Peripherals.** Peripherals are posters, signs, or tabletop displays placed around the classroom. Peripherals can list definitions, show relationships, explain the steps in a process, or graphically represent content material. Any time students are in the room surrounded by these peripherals, they will be learning. Refer to the peripherals during class presentations and encourage students to use them to preview, learn, or review information. "Most of what the brain learns is nonconscious. In fact, studies done on the impact of peripherals . . . suggest that they are much more powerful influences on the brain than previously thought. After two weeks, the effects of direct instruction have diminished. But the effects of peripherals often go up!" (Jensen, 1997, p. 19)

**Model Presentation.** Prepare for your lesson by building a model of a process, an abstract concept, or another central aspect of your unit. Use cardboard boxes, foam cups, pieces of poster board, toy-building or modeling materials, or craft materials. Label the different parts of the model or mock-up. As you are presenting your material, build the model for the class piece by piece, explaining the importance of each part. Next, you might take the model apart and have the students put it back together, explaining it as they go, or build a model of their own at their tables (Meier, 1999).

**Mind Maps.** Mind maps are pictorial representations of content that allow the student (or teacher) creating the mind map to generate symbols that represent concrete or abstract information, show relationships, depict chronological events, or list the steps of a process in a way that is meaningful to her. You might want to begin using mind maps by creating one yourself and having students label and color it as you explain the various parts. Next, generate one with the class as you present new material. Finally, encourage students to make mind maps on their own. Some of the keys to effective minds maps are that they are primarily made up of symbols rather than words, appropriate colors are used to help bring meaning to the various symbols, and relationships and steps are clearly depicted through the use of arrows and other visual devices.

**Graphic Organizers.** Graphic organizers are visual representations of principles, abstract concepts, and relationships. According to the Dimensions of Learning model, "most declarative information can be organized into one of . . . six patterns: descriptions, time sequences, process-cause-effect relationships, episodes, generalizations/principles, or concepts. Each of these organizational patterns can be depicted in a graphic organizer that can be used in the classroom in two ways: in teacher-structured and student-structured lessons" (Marzano & Pickering, 1997, p. 62). If the teacher has organized the material into a pattern during his planning, he can present the material to the students using the appropriate graphic organizer. Once the students are comfortable with using graphic organizers, the teacher can provide the information to the students individually, in pairs, or in small groups, and ask them to choose and complete the appropriate graphic organizer.

**Group Mural.** To create a class or group mural, give individuals, pairs, or triads a topic to research using the resources available in the room. Tape a long strip of roll paper to the wall and ask the students to create a picture or image that summarizes or illustrates the topic on a section of the paper. When the drawing is complete, ask each creator to briefly explain the drawing and what it represents. Fill in any points that the learners missed about the topics. You might do this before a lesson without the resources to discover any prior knowledge on a particular topic, as part of the lesson to engage the students in both teaching and learning the content, or after the lesson as a review and formative assessment (Meier, 1999).

**Link Strategy.** The link strategy relies on a mental picture to help students remember course content, linking one image to another in a chain or a story. The link strategy is particularly useful for rote memorization. I'm not in favor of having students memorize a great deal of information that they could easily look up, but many state tests demand that certain information be memorized by all students. Dimensions of Learning gives a great example of a link strategy to use if students are required to memorize the 13 original colonies: Georgia, New Jersey, Delaware, New York, North Carolina, South Carolina, Virginia, New Hampshire, Pennsylvania, Connecticut, Rhode Island, Maryland, and Massachusetts:

For example, the student might first picture Georgette (Georgia), the Jersey cow (New Jersey). Next she would imagine Georgette the Jersey cow putting on a pair of yellow underwear (which sounds like Delaware) as she stands on top of the Empire State Building (New York). Georgette then begins singing Christmas carols (North and South Carolina). Under her left "arm" Georgia is holding a Virginia ham (Virginia, New Hampshire). In her right "hand" she has a pen. With the pen, Georgette is connecting dots (which sounds like Connecticut). These dots join to form the picture of a road (Rhode Island). On the road is Marilyn Monroe (Maryland) on her way to Sunday mass (Massachusetts). (Marzano & Pickering, 1997, p. 75)

At first, you might ask if it wouldn't be easier to just memorize a list of the states. Actually, it isn't. The mental image, which only takes two or three repetitions with the students, stays with them. A list of the states might take 30 to 40 repetitions. You can create linked stories like this for other information that your students may be required to memorize, or you might engage them in creating the images themselves.

**Rhyming Peg Word.** The rhyming peg word strategy uses both auditory and visual memory to help students remember information that is organized in a list format. This strategy begins by visualizing the following rhymes:

- 1 is a bun.
- 2 is a shoe.
- 3 is a tree.
- 4 is a door.
- 5 is a hive.
- 6 is a pile of sticks.
- 7 is heaven.
- 8 is a gate.
- 9 is a line.
- 10 is a hen.

The words *bun, shoe, tree,* and so on are easy to remember because they rhyme with the numbers 1 though 10. "If a student wants to put information in slot #1 (1 is a bun) of the framework, she would do so by forming a mental image of the information she wants to remember that also includes a bun, because 'bun' is the peg word for the first slot of the framework" (Marzano & Pickering, 1997, p. 76).

For example, assume the student wants to memorize seven different life zones, or biomes:

- broadleaf forest
- hot desert
- tropical rainforest
- needle-leaf forest
- tundra
- mountain
- dry woodland

The student might begin by picturing a broad oak leaf inside a hamburger bun, placing that mental image in Slot 1 of the framework. In Slot 2, the student might imagine a shoe filled with hot sand, representing the hot desert biome. To remember the tropical rainforest, the student might imagine a huge tree (Slot 3) with rain dripping from its leaves. In Slot 4, the student might picture a door that weighs a ton opening out into a world of frozen soil and moss to remember the tundra biome. The image of a huge beehive at the summit of a mountain could be put in Slot 5. Imagining a forest made of dry sticks would help the student remember dry woodland in Slot 6. And finally, the image of the sun shining through a pine forest filled with angels playing harps could be placed in Slot 7 (heaven).

I would like to reiterate that I don't recommend that teachers require students to memorize information that they could easily look up, but the reality is that a number of state and other standardized assessments still ask students to commit information to memory. The rhyming peg word strategy can help students be more successful in those situations. This strategy has other practical uses, however. I often use it to remember shopping lists if I don't have a pen or paper to write down the items I need. It works!

**Living Props.** This strategy is primarily visual, but is also somatic and auditory. Before the lesson, the teacher makes signs or three-dimensional objects that represent concepts, steps in a process, or components of a system. When you are ready to present the lesson, ask a small group of volunteers to come to the front of the room. Have each volunteer hold or wear one of these objects as you give a presentation on the topic. Ask the volunteers to act out the process or system as you describe it. A middle school English teacher I observed used this strategy to teach the writing process. Students were asked to wear large nametags that said: "brainstorming," "organizing," "drafting," "revising," "final draft," and "publishing." The first student, "brainstorming," was given a bag with 20 or so building blocks in it. While the teacher explained the brainstorming process, this student tossed all the blocks out onto a 4' x 4' piece of felt. The "organizing" student then put these blocks into an organized pattern, tossing a few of the blocks back into the bag while the teacher explained the process of outlining and mental mapping. When the teacher explained drafting, the student wearing the "drafting" nametag took the organized pattern of blocks and put them into the shape of a paragraph. The "revising" student rearranged a few blocks, tossing out a couple more into the bag, as the teacher explained the editing process. The "final drafting" student mimed the process of writing and gestured to the final pattern of blocks, and the "publishing" student gestured to the class an invitation to "read" the final work. Everyone in the class enjoyed the lesson, and everyone had a better idea of what the writing process entailed.

**Instructor Role Play.** Prepare a skit, role play, or simulation involving either material to be reviewed or newly introduced information. During class, act out the role play for learners. You may need to ask a colleague or a student to help you, briefing him beforehand. After the role play, direct the students to ask or answer questions about what they just saw. Afterward, discuss the important issues or topics that were raised during the role play. A middle school science teacher used this strategy to introduce the scientific method; he conducted a simple experiment for the class, thinking aloud as he went through the steps from hypothesis to conclusion. In an interesting variation, he did the process the wrong way, coming up with a humorous and preposterous conclusion; then he did it the right way. The questions he asked afterward helped the students generate the steps in the scientific process of experimentation (Meier, 1999).

**Props to Illustrate Concepts.** Like the building blocks used in Living Props to symbolize ideas in a student paragraph or essay, all kinds of physical objects can be used to represent the concepts and processes you are trying to teach. You can gather toys, garage sale items, or common household objects and use them during your presentations or demonstrations to make ideas more vivid, concrete, and memorable. Hand puppets can represent fictional or historic characters. Slinky toys are often used to demonstrate wave patterns in physics. Think of some objects you can use to build mock-ups or use as metaphors to illustrate your content.

**Information Doodles.** For effective learning to take place, students need to process the information they've been presented on a regular basis. One way to give students the opportunity is to pause during a presentation or lecture and ask the learners to draw a picture, cartoon, or symbol of the most important things they've just learned. Next, they turn to a partner and explain their doodles. Finally, ask volunteers to show and explain their doodles to the whole class. You might post the doodles on the wall and encourage students to look at one another's doodles during a brief break (Meier, 1999).

## Intellectual

Besides appealing to the somatic, auditory, and visual learning modes, teachers need to appeal to the intellect for effective learning to take place. Dave Meier of the Center for Accelerated Learning explains:

> By intellectual, we do not mean the emotionless, disconnected, rationalistic, academic, compartmentalized, and exclusively "left brain" approach to education learning so characteristic of Western education. What the term "intellectual" means . . . is the exercise of internal intelligence of the human mind/body as it reflects on its experience and creates connections, meanings, plans, and values out of it. To be active, the intellectual mind requires no additional information from the senses, but is able to create meaning out of what its senses have already presented to it. (1999)

In discussing the SAVI approach, we have focused on helping the brain gather information through the various senses, with some intellectual processing involved in most of the activities. In this section, we focus on strategies that engage the function of the neocortex (the reasoning part of the brain) in making connections and building meaning.

**Collaborative Pretest.** Giving students opportunities to discover and discuss what they already know about a given topic or process helps them learn something new, giving them, in a sense, a "hook" on which to hang the new information. Some of the strategies that we've already discussed are intended to do just that. For example, the KWL strategy begins with the question, "What do you already *know* about . . . ?" Meier suggests starting with a collaborative pretest. The teacher prepares a list of true or false, multiple-choice, or short-answer questions before class. At the beginning of class, students are told to collaborate to find the answers. The collaboration encourages students to verbally process their prior knowledge. You might play music quietly in the background. Once completed, quickly go over the test together, encouraging every student to answer a question out loud.

**Student-Generated Questions.** Another way to create a "hook" in the brain for new information is have students develop questions about the upcoming topic. Jensen states:

> When it comes to learning, the brain is more receptive to questions than answers. Why? It seems that two things occur: (1) Curiosity is a distinct physiological state. It triggers changes in our posture, eye movements, and promotes the chemical reactions that are advantageous to better arousal, learning, and recall. (2) When we ask a question of ourselves, the brain will continue to process even after we have come up with an answer. To your brain, the process is far more important than the answer. (1997, p. 25)

The W of the KWL strategy is "What do you *want* to learn about . . . ?" This is one method of getting students to generate questions. Sometimes, unfortunately, the answer comes in the form of a loud, unanimous "Nothing!" One way to avoid that is to have the students, individually or in pairs, generate questions they could ask about the topic. They can then put the questions up on the wall to refer to during the lesson or unit, publish them, or put them on tape. You might even hold a contest, having the students vote on the best or most thought-provoking questions. (Give them each two votes, one for their own if they wish and one for someone else's.) You could trade questions with other teachers, have a Question of the Day board, or put the questions in a hat and have a daily drawing. Make asking questions a part of your classroom culture.

**Thematic Integrated Units.** The brain learns poorly when we attempt to learn one topic or one part of a topic separately. According to Jensen:

> Imagine trying to learn to ride a bicycle by taking classes in mechanics, road safety, neighborhood geography . . . first aid, and courage. We'd never even want to try it and we certainly wouldn't enjoy the process. Instead, most of us just jumped on a bicycle and [with guidance] tried it out. (1997, p. 11)

The brain learns best when it is allowed to make connections between a variety of bits of information and subject areas in a real-world context. Here are some of Jensen's suggestions:

1.  Use a concept as an umbrella theme for an integrated unit. Topics such as "patterns," "change," "perspectives," or "growth" can easily be brought into all subject areas to help students make connections. For example, under the theme of "patterns," students could study geometric patterns in mathematics. In English, students could study patterns of sounds and rhythms in poetry. In social studies, population patterns might be the topic. In languages other than English, one could study patterns in syntax or in verb conjugation. In science, students might look at evolutionary patterns. Studying patterns of composition in music or art composition might be another way of helping students make interdisciplinary connections.

2.  Give students real-world projects. In math, it could be as simple as figuring out the cost of school cleaning supplies for a year or as complex as studying financial planning. In geography, it could be planning a trip around the world. In science, it could be determining the population and species of animals that live in a patch of woods

behind the school. In languages other than English, it might be creating tourist guides in the topic language.

3. Stay with a theme topic, but go off on interdisciplinary tangents. "For example, studying about a river can mean learning about its history, geography, ecology, cultures, etc." (Jensen, 1997, p. 11)

**Pulse Learning.** Using this strategy, the learner is provided with a "pulse" of focused learning, in which the brain's attention is on the external world, followed by diffused learning, in which the brain's attention is on the inner world. Jensen discusses the basis for this strategy:

> The human brain is not designed for continuous learning. That's because the brain needs processing time and "down time" away from directed, focused learning. You can either have your learners' attention or they can be making meaning, but you can't have both at once. The best learning occurs with alternating cycles of focus, diffusion, focus, and diffusion. Focused learning is continued, directed attention with minimal learner choice. Examples include presenter lectures or active discussions. Diffusion is unfocused, positive choice time where the learner may be journaling, having partner discussions, using think time, or doing projects. (1997, p. 25)

Focused activities should be relatively short. A good rule of thumb is that focused learning should last no longer in minutes than the age of the student, with the maximum focus time for any age being about 20 minutes. The focused learning should be followed by 2 to 5 minutes of diffused learning. Plan each lesson so that you have both kinds of learning, creating a natural pulse for your learners' brains.

**The Three-Minute Pause.** One way of creating pulse learning is to use this strategy. "Jay McTighe of the Maryland Assessment Consortium recommends that teachers regularly use the three-minute pause. This means stopping every 10 or 15 minutes during a classroom activity and asking students to reflect on and verbalize about something they have learned" (Marzano & Pickering, 1997, p. 53). This strategy is an excellent way to help students make connections to their own lives or to make meaning out of a manageable amount of new learning. Some prompts to help structure the three-minute pause include the following:

1. How does this information relate to you?
2. Summarize what you've just learned in your own words.
3. How does what we've just learned relate to . . . ?
4. How is what we've just discussed similar or different from . . . ?
5. Identify one thing that you already knew and one thing that was new to you.

**Learning Journals.** Another strategy teachers can employ to create pulse learning is the learning journal. After direct instruction or another focused learning activity, teachers can ask their students to turn to their journals to create their own meaning about the information they've just learned or the activity they've just experienced. Jensen lists three things that make information meaningful to the brain:

1. Putting information together to make a pattern, to understand relationships and connections;
2. That which stimulates emotions, either positively or negatively; and
3. That which impacts the learner's personal life. (1997, p. 13)

Journal prompts that address these things can help students internalize the learning. Some suggestions are to

1. Ask students to make connections between what they've just learned or experienced and previous knowledge;
2. Ask students to make connections between the content they've just learned and another subject area;
3. Ask students how they would feel if they were in the same situation as the literary character, historical figure, or scientist they've just learned about;
4. Have students write about the feelings they experienced during the learning activity;
5. "Tie the learning into closely held personal values of the learners: security for younger learners, peer acceptance and identity for

adolescents, respect and achievement for older students" (Jensen, 1997, p. 13); and

6. Ask learners to list three ways they can relate the learning to their own lives. It could be through travel they've done or something from TV, movies, music, or their own life experience.

**Presentation Roulette.** Have students work in pairs, assigning each pair a number. After teaching a manageable chunk of information, pause and ask the students to turn to their partner and summarize what they've just learned or make a connection to something they've previously learned. After a minute or two, pull a number out of a hat and have that pair stand up and summarize the material or share the connection they've just made. Comment as necessary and go on. This will keep all the students engaged in the direct instruction, make them accountable for the learning, and help them make meaning of the information you're presenting (Meier, 1999).

**Collaborative Definitions.** Write several concepts or terms on a flipchart or transparency. Show the list to teams of students and have them research definitions for the terms and put them in their own words. Have the teams present their definitions, correcting or enhancing them as necessary (Meier, 1999).

**Pair Teaching.** Have everyone prepare a one-minute review with a partner on something they've learned during the lesson or the unit. Choose pairs to come up in front of the class by random, by numbers, or by volunteering. Make sure there is a timekeeper to ensure that the pairs adhere to the one-minute time limit, using the entire minute but not going over. When each pair is finished, you might let them choose the next pair (Jensen, 1997).

## Assessment

If you provide students with an engaging curriculum of essential knowledge and skills, help them see that the work that they are being asked to do is useful, and provide instruction that appeals to a variety of learning modalities and is compatible with the way the brain learns, you've done a great deal to ensure student success in your classroom. If you go one more step and use effective assessment practices, you are virtually guaranteeing success for all students. In this section, we will examine three assessment strategies you can use to raise student achievement in your classroom: alignment, providing choices of assessment tools, and creating a competency-based classroom.

## Alignment

One of the best ways to ensure student success on the summative assessment is to follow the advice that Steven Covey provides in *The Seven Habits of Highly Effective People* (1989). Habit Two says that highly effective people, "Begin with the end in mind" (p. 95). In planning an instructional unit, that would mean that the teacher would begin by

- Identifying the main concept that the unit will focus on. Concepts help to arouse students' interest—by giving them a "hook" to connect the new knowledge to their lives and experience—and to unify all the knowledge and skills in the unit. Using a unifying concept helps teachers focus a unit that might otherwise include too much disjointed or unnecessary content. Some examples of concepts are previously listed in the Intellectual section of SAVI learning. One way to identify a concept underlying a given content area topic would be to fill in the blanks: _____ is a study in _____. Your topic would be in the first blank, the related concept would be in the second. If, for example, you were going to teach a novel and focus on how character change helps us understand the novel's theme, your main concept might be "change." For a "hook," you might bring in a willing accomplice and tell the class that starting tomorrow, Ms. Jones will be taking over the class. Next, you might have Ms. Jones explain to the class, "There will be a few changes made around here in the way we do things," and go on to explain all the changes, from seating assignments to class policies and procedures. Following up this experience with a discussion of how change affects us could lead into another discussion about change that has occurred in the students' lives. Having experienced the concept you'll be focusing on and having had a chance to connect it to their lives, the students are now ready to learn the content you want to teach!

- Mind-mapping all the knowledge and skills that must be taught and learned in the unit. Place the general topic of the unit in a circle in the middle of a piece of paper and identify all the subtopics and skills that are essential for your students to know and be able to do by the end of that unit (see Figure 5.1).

- Devising assessment tools that would measure that particular knowledge and set of skills. You will undoubtedly need to create some formative assessments: quizzes, informal individual or group discussions, journal entries, and so on. These formative assessments help you determine whether your students are learning what you think they should be learning, and will help you decide when they are ready for the summative assessment, which is the final evaluation tool you'll use to assess their learning. It is critical to closely analyze your assessment tool, making sure it measures the knowledge and skills you intended to measure, not some additional information or skill that you didn't teach.

## Assessment Choices

Everyone knows that different people have different talents. Howard Gardner has changed the way we look at these talents, calling them "intelligences." He chose the word *intelligence* to make a point with those who "consider logical reasoning or linguistic competence to be on a different plane" than other ways of being smart (1993, p. 35). In his book *Multiple Intelligences: The Theory in Practice*, Gardner lists seven kinds of intelligence:

- *Musical*—The ability to produce and appreciate rhythm, pitch, and timbre; appreciation of the forms of musical expressiveness.

- *Body-Kinesthetic*—The ability to control one's body movements and to handle objects skillfully.

- *Logical-Mathematical*—The sensitivity to, and capacity to discern logical or numerical patterns; the ability to handle long chains of reasoning.

- *Linguistic*—Sensitivity to the sounds, structure, meanings, and functions of words and language.
- *Spacial*—The capacity to perceive the visual-spacial world accurately and to perform transformations on one's initial perceptions.
- *Interpersonal*—The capacity to discern and respond appropriately to the moods, temperaments, motivations, and desires of other people.
- *Intrapersonal*—Having access to one's own inner life and the ability to discriminate among one's emotions; knowledge of one's own strengths and weaknesses.

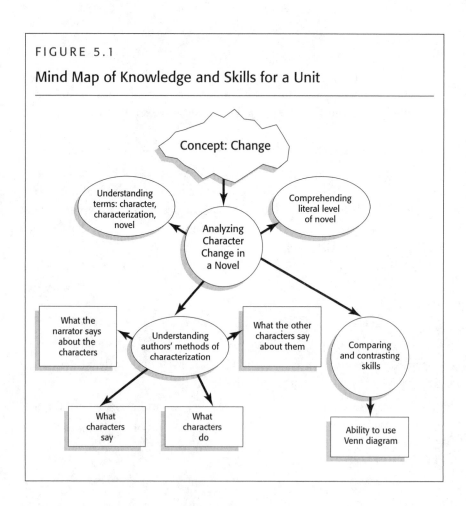

FIGURE 5.1

**Mind Map of Knowledge and Skills for a Unit**

The implications of the theory in regard to assessment are significant. If we want to help our students meet their need for power, we need to allow them to use their individual strengths, their intelligences, to show us what they have learned. Asking a student whose primary intelligence is musical or body-kinesthetic to perform only assessments that are logical-mathematic puts that student at a disadvantage. There may be other ways that particular student could use his talents to demonstrate his learning that would satisfy both the teacher and the student. Chapter 6 lists more than 100 assessment devices that you might use to give your students more choices in how they are evaluated.

There are times that providing choices of assessment is not an option. For example, if you want the students to be able to compute the area of a circle, the logical-mathematical test is probably the only choice. If you want students to learn to write a clear, well-supported paragraph, then writing paragraphs is, of course, the best choice. If, on the other hand, the learning is more content-based, more knowledge than skill, you may find that students can demonstrate that knowledge in many ways. In my English classroom, for example, I often wanted my students to demonstrate their learning by writing a certain kind of essay. However, I also wanted to allow my students to demonstrate their learning in ways that appealed to their talents. One of those times was at the end of the unit on John Gardner's novel *Grendel*. I wanted students to demonstrate an understanding of

- The literal level of the novel,
- Gardner's characterization of one of the central figures in the novel,
- The novel's theme, and
- How character development helps reveal a novel's theme.

Having explained the assessment criteria to the students, I gave them a list of possible assessment devices they could choose from, but told them that if they came up with one that was not on the list, they could use it as long as they discussed it with me and it satisfied the criteria.

The projects that the students did were wonderful. Some chose to use their verbal-linguistic and interpersonal intelligences and write character and thematic analysis essays. One girl chose to use her spatial intelligence, create a sculpture, and explain it to the class. Another student decided to use his musical intelligence by writing and performing "The Ballad of Grendel" for the class. A pair of students developed a giant board game that took up the whole classroom floor, which we then played. Another team of students got together and performed a skit of Grendel's funeral, each playing a character, giving a eulogy in character, meeting all the criteria, and providing the class with a lot of laughs. Each project demonstrated their learning, allowed them to use their preferred intelligence, and provided us all with novelty within the structure of the classroom. It was great! As long as you are clear about the information or concepts you want your students to demonstrate by providing them with a checklist of the criteria for the assessment, you can empower your students by giving them choices in how they demonstrate their learning.

## The Competence-Based Classroom (CBC)

When I was a classroom teacher, I asked my students, "When you go to dinner before the senior prom, do you want to go to an A+ restaurant or a D restaurant? How about when you get your hair cut? Do you want to go to a hair stylist who got at least a B in school, or one who got a 65? When you buy a car, do you want one assembled by an A assembler or one who does just the bare minimum to get paid, maybe a C?" My students were unanimous in their answers that they wouldn't want to frequent any business that didn't do competent work. They also agreed that competent work would earn at least a B. In the real world, we expect people to be competent at their jobs, and we try to frequent only those businesses that do competent, high-quality work. In many of Glasser's writings and in many of his presentations, he makes the point that a student can go through 13 years of school and graduate without doing one bit of competent work, achieving Cs and Ds all along the way—hardly what anyone would call competence. As Glasser says in *Every Student Can Succeed*, to "give credit for less than competence, dooms most students to incompetence" (2000b, p. 85). In the workplace, incompetent workers are discharged or not promoted. "But in school, students are not discharged for incompetence, nor should they be. Instead we should make a serious effort to move them to competence instead of what we are doing now, which is social promotion" (p. 86).

If teachers do not help their students meet their power need by help-ing them achieve competence, they are not only doing a disservice to the children who are doing less-than-competent work, they are also causing problems for themselves and the other students in the class-room. As Glasser states:

> The discipline problems you face in your classroom are caused by stu-dents who are not succeeding in school. They know what school success is and they've given up on the idea they'll succeed. Since you're the teacher, they tend to blame you for their lack of success and they're rebelling against you, the schoolwork and the school . . . If you adopt the CBC [competence-based classroom], they'll discover that school success is possible.(2000b, p. 65)

How does one move from the traditional practices that produced the well-known "normal" distribution curve, the bell curve, to a compe-tence-based classroom approach that would move all students toward the A and B end of the scale? Fortunately, the idea of the competence-based classroom is not new. It's been around since Benjamin Bloom out-lined his thesis in an important article titled "Learning for Mastery" (1968). Mastery learning, another name for the competence-based classroom, is thoroughly examined and explained by Ellis and Fouts in *Research on Educational Innovations* (1997). The authors explain that mastery learning can be implemented in classrooms of 30 or so in a vari-ety of ways. "One answer could be found in peer teaching. Another could be found in cooperative learning" (p.182). According to Ellis and Fouts, mostly group-based mastery learning has been carried out using the following components:

- *Planning*—Content or skill to be learned is analyzed and divided into small units with related specific objectives and performance criteria. Pre-instruction assessment identifies instructional starting point.

- *Instruction*—Teachers use appropriate strategies based on careful sequencing of the learning. In many instances, direct instruction is used involving modeling and practice.

- *Formative Evaluation*—Assessment is frequently used throughout the instructional process to determine if the learner is mastering the sequential prerequisite skills.

- *Correctives and Enrichment*—Based on the formative evaluation results, the students who have not achieved mastery are provided with feedback and the material is re-taught using alternative instructional approaches or examples and with additional practice. Students who have mastered the material are provided with individual enrichment activities that help them extend and broaden their learning.

- *Final Evaluation*—Assessment to determine the degree to which the new content or skills have been mastered. This is repeated as necessary. (pp. 183–184)

Some argue that reteaching and retesting are not realistic, not the way the real world works. I disagree. If someone fails their road test for their driver's license, they are allowed to take the test as many times as necessary to demonstrate their competence. The same is true for most state bar examinations. In the real world, there are lots of second chances. Why not in schools?

In my own classroom, I found that when I required competence (mastery) on important assignments, students met my expectations. When I first introduced the practice, some of my students tested my resolve by handing in the same incompetent work that they'd become accustomed to. When they got their papers back with no grade, just some specific comments throughout and a note saying, "Rewrite" or "Not Yet" at the top, they grumbled things like, "What's with this guy? I've never gotten anything higher than a C on an essay in my life." Some students went so far as to beg for a 0. When I explained to them that to get credit for the class, they needed to achieve a B or better, some went so far as to wait for the report card to see if I meant it. I did. The first year I tried this, it took lots of discussion and lots of commitment to the concept of the CBC.

It seemed at times that it would have been easier to just give them the Cs, Ds, and Fs that many had received in the past and had grown accustomed to and move on to a new topic. It was all worth it, however, when the student who had "never gotten anything higher than a C on an essay" in his life walked out of my classroom with an A paper, his back straight with a look on his face of sheer pride. Even though that high school senior was 18 years old, I'd bet $100 that his essay went up on the refrigerator at home that evening. The next year it was easier. Brothers and sisters tend to spread the word: "When Erwin tells you that you gotta get a B or better on an assignment, he really means it." The students understood that it was for their benefit. There were fewer rewrites and retests, and fewer kids tested my resolve. I learned that you can't reteach and reassess every little quiz or homework assignment, but if the major summative assessments are indeed evaluating important, useful information and skills, they're important enough to provide students with second chances.

My experience is simply anecdotal evidence. Fortunately, you don't have to base your classroom practices on my experience only. There is a significant amount of research supporting the practice of mastery learning. According to *Research on Educational Innovations*, "the research on mastery learning is about as strong as one can find in the annals of educational investigation. Study after study indicates the superiority of mastery learning over traditional methods" (Ellis & Fouts, 1997, p. 185). In "Syntheses of Research on Mastery Learning," a meta-analysis of the research that has been done on mastery learning since its introduction in the 1960s, Stephen Anderson finds that "a majority of studies showed that mastery learning has a positive effect on achievement at all levels and for all subjects and results in positive affective outcomes for students and teachers" (1994, p. 1). Anderson's research supports Bloom's assertion, in his introduction to Thomas Guskey's *Implementing Mastery Learning*, that mastery learning has made "positive contributions to school achievement as well as to the learners' feelings about themselves and school learning" (1997, p. 4).

## Conclusions

In any organization, whenever someone gains knowledge or skills and is given opportunities to maximize his potential, the whole organization gains. Similarly, in a classroom, as each student gains power in responsible ways, the whole class is empowered, particularly the teacher. By providing a curriculum that students understand to be useful, by teaching in ways that are compatible with the way the brain learns, and by allowing students to demonstrate their knowledge and skills in a variety of ways, teachers are creating the conditions for high quality learning, better student achievement, and greater success for all students. Further, by giving students more than one chance to demonstrate what they know and can do, teachers avoid creating "curriculum casualties" (Hargis, 1995, p. 66): students who fall through the cracks and experience academic and behavioral problems while in school and often become problems for society at large once they leave. By intentionally increasing the effectiveness of our curriculum, instructional strategies, and assessment, we are providing students with the capacity to create a better world for everyone. Now that's power!

# 6

# Freedom in the Classroom

*These things shall be—a loftier race*
*Than e'er the world hath known shall rise*
*With flame of freedom in their souls*
*And light of knowledge in their eyes.*
                    *—John Addington Symonds,*
                    *"The Days That Are to Be"*

"MY CLASSROOM IS NOT A DEMOCRACY!" I OVERHEARD ONE SOCIAL STUDIES
teacher exclaim to another during a break in a workshop I recently
taught. "And there is only one rule: Do what I tell you to do." How
ironic, I thought, that in a country founded on the idea of preserving the
"inalienable rights" of "life, liberty, and the pursuit of happiness" that a
teacher of American history, of all subjects, would utter such a statement. Ironic, maybe, but it's not unheard of. There are probably thousands of tiny totalitarian regimes in schools all over the world. In fact, if
you were to ask students where they have freedom in school, you would
frequently hear, "We don't!" Granted, some of what these students say is
for effect, yet some is based in reality.

Freedom may be one of the more difficult of the basic needs for students to meet in school; but if we hope to help students become responsible members of a democratic society, then it is important that we allow

149

them to experience freedom in their formative years. When I talk about freedom, I'm not saying we give students carte blanche or have an "anything-goes-as-long-as-you're-meeting-your-needs" attitude. That is known as *license*, freedom without responsibility. In schools, as in society, each measure of freedom we exercise comes with an equal portion of responsibility. If we hope students will leave school having the strength to enjoy freedom responsibly, we must create circumstances that will allow them to exercise those "muscles" frequently and consistently.

In this chapter, we will be considering two kinds of freedom: *freedom from* and *freedom to*. *Freedom from* refers to opportunities that allow us to experience a needed change or to avoid an unpleasant situation. For example, some days instead of going for a run on my usual hilly route, I'll drive a few minutes and run on a flat course along a local river. That is *freedom from* my usual routine, which helps prevent boredom, and *freedom from* the unpleasantness that sometimes accompanies hill running. *Freedom to* refers to opportunities that allow us to choose from a variety of options. Receiving a gift certificate to a bookstore provides us with the *freedom to* choose from thousands of titles and find the book just right for us. Some things allow us both *freedom from* and *freedom to*. Going out to dinner, for example, allows us *freedom to* choose where to dine and what to order and *freedom from* preparing a meal and doing dishes.

In the following pages, we will examine classroom practices that provide students with both *freedom from* and *freedom to*. Although many strategies provide both kinds of freedom, I've placed them in one or the other for the sake of organization.

## Practices Granting *Freedom From*

### Novelty

In *Teaching with the Brain in Mind*, Jensen emphasizes the importance of providing a "rich balance of novelty and ritual" (1998, p. 50). By *ritual*, Jensen refers to procedures and routines—structures that are critical to a smooth-running classroom. We examined procedures in Chapter 2 and noted how important they are to the students' survival need, the need for order and a sense of security. Too much of any good thing has its disadvantages, however. If everything we do is structured and predictable, pretty soon the class will be bored to distraction, literally. If we want to gain and keep the students' attention and get them into an optimal learning state, we need to inject novelty into our routine. Some ways of creating novelty are the following:

- Changing location. Teachers can move to a different part of the room during instruction. Students can change seats, move to the back or side of the room, or even go outside for part of a lesson. You might even arrange with another teacher to switch rooms for a day or part of a day.
- Introducing lessons with different kinds of music.
- Using a variety of instructional strategies. Chapter 5 listed dozens of teaching tools that appeal to different learning styles (SAVI).
- Using a variety of cooperative learning structures (see Chapter 3).
- Having students work with a different partner or group.
- Beginning class with a team-building activity (see Chapter 3).
- Inserting an energizer during a lesson (see Chapter 7).
- Using props, noisemakers, costumes, poetry, or singing to get their attention.
- Taking the class on a field trip. Outings are a wonderful way to provide freedom from the daily routine. Relating to a unit of study, field trips can also be a powerful learning strategy, helping students see real-life application of classroom concepts and skills.

Although it is not necessary to turn the classroom into a three-ring circus, it is important for teachers to recognize that changes in the routine are vital to gaining and keeping students' attention.

## Mastery Learning

Previously discussed in Chapter 5 as a means to help students meet their need for power, mastery learning is also a way to help students gain *freedom from* failure. Brain researchers have long known that when the human brain feels threatened, it "downshifts" into survival mode. The two general behavioral options for the brain under the stress of a perceived threat are "fight or flight." Many high-achieving students see the traditional grading system as a reward system. Many other students see it as a threat. Students who feel threatened may choose the "fight" option, which in school manifests itself in acting out, aggression, belligerence, or insubordination. Or they may choose the "flight" option, which is withdrawing, being absent, giving up, or escaping through drugs or alcohol. As Jensen says, "Threats activate defense mechanisms that are great for survival but lousy for learning" (1998, p. 57). If we make the amount of time a student needs to master a concept or a skill the variable instead of the amount of learning, we can reduce the threat of failure and possibly even eliminate it. Let students know at the beginning of the year that you are not interested in failing them, that you are interested in helping them be successful. And that means you will give them second or third chances to demonstrate their competence. Such a discussion alone will go a long way toward reducing the threat of failure. Of course, students will need to see you follow through on that statement, but feeling *free from* the threat of failure will reduce student stress and enhance student learning potential.

## Chill Out Chair

The chill out chair is a comfortable chair where students can choose to sit and calm themselves down when they are upset or angry and are not in an emotional state to be part of the class. It's not a punishment to go to the chill out chair; it's simply an option. When a student wants to indicate that she would like to go to the chill out chair, it's best to have a silent signal of some sort worked out beforehand. The student might flash a peace sign or a referee's time-out signal. With the teacher's permission, the student goes to the chill out chair, calms herself down, and rejoins the class when she is ready. Students can be taught to calm themselves, a skill that may be one of the most useful things they learn in school. Don't try to teach this skill to students when they are upset; do it at a time, preferably at the beginning of the year, when everyone is behaving genially. Teach students to

1. Remove themselves physically from the stressful situation, if possible.

2. Breathe slowly and deeply, counting their breath for 10 to 15 inhalation-exhalation cycles.
3. Continue to breathe slowly and silently, now repeating a pleasant thought over and over.

Have students practice this calming exercise at their desks so they'll be able to use it when they face an emotionally difficult situation. The pleasant thought will vary from student to student, but examples some students have shared with me are "My dog Chester loves me," "I love to snowmobile," and "Saturday I can play outside all day." Other students create a pleasant mental picture (their room, the beach, a forest path, a burning candle) and focus on that. The option of going to the chill out chair offers students *freedom from* having to participate in class when they are not emotionally ready, which also gives them *freedom from* being assigned a detention or kicked out of class for nonparticipation. Of course, some students may try to abuse the privilege of the chill out chair at first. By conferencing with those students as soon as you observe the problem, you can prevent further misuse. Also, you may occasionally invite a student to use the chill out chair to prevent having to send him to the office or time-out room.

## Practices Granting *Freedom To*

### Choice of Seats

Allowing students to choose where they sit is one way to help them meet their *freedom to* need. The responsibility that comes with this freedom must be discussed with the students. It's important that they understand that if they are going to choose to sit near their friends, they are expected to be respectful of you and the rest of the class and not engage in side conversations. Also, it should be clear that if they do, you have the prerogative of moving their seats. Jensen discusses the importance of providing students with opportunities for variety and choice in where they position themselves for learning: "The kinesthetic-tactile learners may need to stand, move, sit on the floor, or walk around at times. Some are visual learners who want to sit up front or near the best 'show' in the room. . . . The side of the room affects learning, too.

Learners in the presenter's left side will be taking in information more dominantly in their right hemisphere and vice versa" (1997, p. 65).

## Daily or Weekly Agenda

There may be times when you have a number of things you want to accomplish during a particular day or week, but you can be flexible about when they might be done. Allowing students to help develop the agenda is a simple way of giving them a say in what they will be doing while they *have* to be in school. Knowing what to expect during the school day or week also helps students lower their stress level, further increasing the likelihood of quality learning.

## Choice of Partners or Team Members

Although many times you will want to determine who works with whom in partners or teams (see Chapter 3 on ways of pairing students up), sometimes you may want to give students *freedom to* choose their partners or teammates. After some frustrating experiences with allowing students to choose their own groups, I found a way that worked for me. At the beginning of the year, I had my students take some diagnostic tests: one determining their learning preference (auditory, visual, kinesthetic), one that determined their working style (abstract random, concrete sequential), and a personality inventory that determined whether they were introverted or extraverted. These diagnostics helped me understand the various learning needs of my students, but also came in handy when I had them develop their own learning teams. (You can obtain diagnostic tests like these from major bookstores and career development centers.) A few students volunteered to compile the results of the diagnostic tests, and we posted them on the wall. When it came time to create our teams, the rule was *diversity*. I wanted them to have as many different learning styles, working styles, and personality types as possible. I also encouraged gender diversity. Before they submitted their learning team membership for my approval, they were asked to self-assess. After the teams were chosen, we talked about why I chose the diversity rule and discussed how it could enhance their groups' effectiveness if members were encouraged to play to their strengths. It's not absolutely necessary to go through the process I did when having students choose their teams. It is worthwhile, however, to discuss criteria they might consider in choosing their group members.

## Student-Generated Curriculum

Getting the students involved in developing their own course of study, discussed in Chapter 5, is one of the most effective ways to help students meet their need for freedom while simultaneously tapping into a vast source of intrinsic motivation, student curiosity. In *The Schools Our Children Deserve*, Kohn (1999) describes how one teacher brings this about:

> At the beginning of the year, students are asked to list all the questions they have about themselves (How long will I live? Will I be like my parents?), after which they meet in groups to share their individual lists and look for areas that overlap. Then they repeat the process for questions they have about the world (Why do people hate each other? How did religions evolve?), again listing them individually before finding areas in common—and, with the teacher's help, design units of study to answer their questions. These investigations, on themes such as "Living in the Future" or "Conflicts and Violence," form the basis for the entire year's course of study, requiring the students to draw as necessary from (and weave together) virtually all the conventional disciplines. (p. 149–150)

Granted, on one hand it may be risky allowing students to develop their own units of study, especially in these days of higher standards and more accountability. On the other hand, in what circumstances are students liable to learn more: when they generate the questions, or when the teacher (or the district or state) does? Also, who is more accountable for learning than those who create the curriculum? It's true that students may not have the resources to ask all the "right" questions, but once the students are engaged in a subject they're interested in, the teacher can insert related standards-based curricula without diminishing the students' enthusiasm. It's a win-win situation. For example, Bambi Powers, a 4th grade teacher in Watkins Glen, New York, developed a whole life science unit, the content of which is already part of the state curriculum, on a question her students were curious about: "Why is it that worms are all over the roads and driveways after it rains?" Studying the part worms play in the life cycle, if introduced by the teacher, may have resulted in one big class yawn, but because the topic came from the students, they were totally engaged.

If you're not comfortable with as open-ended an approach as Kohn discusses, you might try what a teacher in Texas did with his middle school science students:

> He didn't ask the students whether they wanted to learn about the whole topic, but he did introduce [a unit on atoms and molecules] by inviting them to look through books on the subject and list questions that occurred to them. The students then came together and constructed a master list, sorting the questions by category and deciding which ones they most wanted answered. The whole lesson took off from there, even though some of the questions were so tough that outside resources had to be brought in to answer them. (Kohn, 1999, p. 152)

If one of our goals as educators is to develop a love of learning in our students that will last into adulthood, allowing them the freedom to construct their own curriculum while still in school just makes sense.

## Order of Learning Units

Your course may be strictly dictated by your school district or state curriculum, making a student-generated curriculum more difficult. One way of providing students with some freedom, even in more restrictive circumstances, is to engage them in choosing the order of topics or units. You might begin by providing the students with a list and briefly explaining the topics you will be studying during the year. If there are 10 general topics, have the students write down a number (1–10) next to each topic. Next, get a volunteer from the class to come up and record the numbers on the board or overhead next to each topic. Have students add up the figures. The topic with the lowest sum would be first, the highest last, and so on. In a high school English class, you could do the same thing with novels. If, for example, you have class sets of eight novels, you might have the students choose the five they prefer to read during the year. In the psychology elective I taught, I would list and explain all the topics we could choose to study during the semester, and have them choose the six that the class found most interesting. They also were required to do an independent inquiry, so if one of their favorite topics wasn't chosen, they could study that area independently.

## Choices Within Assignments

Even limited choices are better than none at all. So you might allow students to choose between two or three essay topics that all demonstrate the learning objective or choose between answering all the odd or even number problems in the textbook. If you are requiring an outside reading assignment, you allow students the freedom to choose any that meet whatever criteria you set.

## Free-Reading Friday

Some elementary and secondary English teachers practice free-reading time. Students can bring in any book that they want on a particular day, and everyone reads silently for an amount of time appropriate to the age of the students. (Rule of thumb: The age of the participants times two equals the maximum number of minutes.) I used to do it on Fridays, but not every Friday. Some schools engage in a practice called "DEAR: Drop Everything And Read" where everyone in the school (teachers, students, secretaries, teacher aides, the principal, and custodians) models the importance of reading by dropping everything they are doing and picking up a book.

## Free Writing

If you use learning journals in your classroom, you might occasionally provide the opportunity for free writing, which enables students to express their thoughts and feelings in a confidential and safe environment. You might give students open-ended topics to give their writing a direction: the future, friendship, family, fun, music, and so on. Or you might just let them write freely about any topic they choose. Free writing can provide a powerful emotional outlet for students, lead to excellent class discussions, and help students generate ideas for formal writing assignments.

*Note:* Preface free writing with a discussion of appropriate versus inappropriate writing content.

## Choice of Performance Assessment

In Chapter 5, I discussed the rationale for and the advantages of allowing students a choice in how they are assessed. If the criteria for mastery or competence is made clear by the teacher and understood by the students, there are dozens of ways students can demonstrate their learning. If the learning you want your students to demonstrate is a particular skill, such as writing a five-paragraph persuasive essay, the choice of assessment is pretty limited. Students will need to write a five-paragraph persuasive essay. They may have a choice regarding the topic, however. If the learning you are assessing is not a specific skill, which is often the case, the choice of assessment is more open-ended. The performance tasks in Figure 6.1 sample some of the ways students can demonstrate their learning in any subject. Some are more appropriate to certain ages than others; some are more suited to certain subjects than others. This alphabetical list is one you can draw upon to offer your students freedom to express their learning in a way that appeals to their strengths.

For each unit you teach, you might provide your students with a list of performance assessment choices that would be appropriate for your students and that particular unit. I often left the door open with the final choice being, "or any other way you can demonstrate the learning criteria, as long as you discuss it with me and we agree on it."

It's also important that students demonstrate their learning in a number of ways throughout the year, so you may encourage students to choose different performance assessments for different learning units.

## Portfolio Choices

Some teachers (and schools) require that their students keep a portfolio in their classes to document academic accomplishments and progress. "Here, students collect what they've done over a period of time, not just because it's helpful to have all that material in one place, but because the process of choosing what to include—and deciding how to

## FIGURE 6.1

## Ways in which students can demonstrate learning

| | | |
|---|---|---|
| Advertisement | Editorial | Outline |
| Advice Column | Essay | Painting |
| Animation | Experiment | Pamphlet |
| Artifact Collection | Fairy Tale | Parody |
| Audiotape | Field Manual | Photo Essay |
| Autobiography | Flip Charts | Play |
| Ballad | Flow Chart | Poem |
| Ballet | Free Verse | Poster |
| Bar Graph | Friendly Letter | Profile |
| Bill-of-Rights | Gallery | Prototype |
| Book Jacket | Game | Puppet Show |
| Book Report | Game Show | Questionnaire |
| Booklet | Graph | Radio Announcement |
| Brochure | Graphic Organizer | Radio Commentary |
| Business Letter | Guidebook | Radio Commercial |
| Campaign Speech | Haiku | Rap Song |
| Cardboard Relief | Handbook | Report |
| Cartoon | Illustration | Research Report |
| CD Cover | Interview | Review |
| Celebrity Profile | Interpretive Dance | Role-Play |
| Chart | Invention | Rubric |
| Characterization | Journal | Satire |
| Cinquain | Learning Center | Science Fiction Story |
| Classification System | Lecture | Scrapbook |
| Classified Ad | Letter to Editor | Sculpture |
| Clothing | Letter of Complaint | Short Story |
| Collage | Letter of Support | Skit |
| Collection | Limerick | Soap Opera |
| Comedy Act | Lyrics | Song |
| Comic Book | Map | Speech |
| Commercial | Memorandum | Survey |
| Costume | Mnemonic | Tall Tale |
| Crossword Puzzle | Mobile | Television Newscast |
| Dance | Model | Television Sitcom |
| Debate | Monologue | 3-D Display |
| Demonstration | Monument | Transparency |
| Diagram | Mural | Toy |
| Dialogue | Music | Translation |
| Diary | Myth | Videotape |
| Diorama | Newsletter | Visual Aid |
| Display | Newspaper | Wall Hanging |
| Documentary | Nursery Rhyme | Year (Decade) in |
| Dramatization | Outline | Review |
| Drawing | Oral Report | Yearbook |

evaluate it—is an opportunity to reflect on their past learning as well as to set new goals" (Kohn, 1999, p. 193). Students may choose what goes in the portfolio to demonstrate improvement over time or to reflect the variety of projects they've accomplished during a period of time. Portfolios provide students with an opportunity to learn to self-evaluate their performance, a skill that will serve them all their lives. And portfolios provide a much more meaningful picture of what a student knows and is able to do than a letter or number on a report card. By using portfolios, students take an active role in their own assessment, just as we hope they will in their own learning.

### Other Choices

In this chapter, I have offered some strategies teachers can use to provide students with choices in the classroom. I would like to challenge you to think of others. Some strategies that I discussed in other chapters also provide students with freedom:

- *Class Meetings* (Chapter 3): Students choose the topic of an open-ended meeting.
- *SAVI Learning* (Chapter 4): Students choose a learning center that appeals to their learning preference (Somatic, Auditory, Visual, or Intellectual).
- *Class Constitution* (Chapter 4): Students choose their own behavioral guidelines.
- *Restroom and Water Passes* (Chapter 2): Students have freedom to go when they need to go.

## Conclusions

Some critics might suggest that by providing students with freedom, we are allowing students to "take over the classroom." That is not what I'm recommending. In the classroom I envision, the teacher is still the manager, the "guide on the side," rather than the authoritarian schoolmaster of the 19th century, the "sage on the stage," if you will. Freedom is an inalienable right, but as John D. Rockefeller Jr. said, "Every right implies a responsibility." Therefore, with every choice our students make, there is an equal measure of responsibility involved. If we truly want students to learn to be responsible decision-makers when they leave school, we must begin to create opportunities for them to make important decisions while they are still in school. But this practice is not about teaching responsibility only; it's also about creating the conditions for learning. "All of us tend to be happiest and most effective when we have some say about what we are doing. If we are instead just told what to do (or in the case of schooling, deprived of any opportunity to make decisions about what [or how] we're learning), achievement tends to drop—right along with any excitement about what we're doing" (Kohn, 1999, p. 150). In classrooms where students are *free from* fear and boredom and *free to* pursue their interests, take risks, and play to their strengths while developing new ones, learning will increase dramatically. Simultaneously, the irresponsible behaviors that some students use in their attempts to meet their freedom need (shouting out answers, walking around the room at inappropriate times, coming in late, failing to complete assignments, and being absent) will significantly decrease.

7

# Fun in the Classroom

*If a man insisted always on being serious, and never allowed himself a bit of fun and relaxation, he would go mad or become unstable without knowing it.*

—Herodotus (c. 485–c. 425 B.C.)

REFLECT FOR A MOMENT ON THE PEOPLE YOU ARE MOST MOTIVATED TO BE WITH, the places where you are most motivated to spend time, the things you are most motivated to do. Without a doubt, these are the people, places, and things that are the most fun. Fun is a great motivator! It's something that all of us want. But it's more than that. Like love and belonging, power, freedom and survival, fun is something we *need*. Most people have not heard the wisdom of Herodotus quoted above, but almost everyone has heard the adage, "All work and no play makes Johnny a dull boy." I'd like to amend the old saying. Not only does it make Johnny or Jenny a dull boy or girl, but all work and no play create the conditions for Johnny and Jenny to be absent, to shut down, to give up, or to disrupt. There seems to be a paradigm in education that fun and learning are opposites. This is completely untrue. If we want students to be motivated to learn, fun must be a regular part of the classroom. Sullo states, "Any inspiring classroom would be characterized by fun. The inspiring teacher intentionally seeks a way to build a sense of joy into the learning plans. To do anything else would be foolish. Can you imagine ever inspiring anyone in a joyless environment?" (1999, p. 37) And as Glasser says, "When we are both learning and having fun, we often look forward to hard work and long hours; without fun these become drudgery" (1984, p. 15).

Many of the strategies discussed in Chapters 2 through 6 help build a sense of fun in the classroom: class-building activities, student-centered curricula, SAVI learning techniques, cooperative learning structures, choices of assessment, and class meetings. Anytime people are effectively meeting one or more of their basic needs, there is a feeling of pleasure. Therefore, it's fun. Although most of the strategies explained in other chapters have a by-product of fun, their chief purpose is to meet one of the other four basic human needs. The strategies in this chapter, however, were deliberately chosen primarily to meet the need for fun. It is essential to understand, however, that though fun (pleasure, laughter, enjoyment) is the principal goal of these activities, other important results can be derived from them. Some of these strategies help build a sense of connectedness and community (love and belonging), many can be used to provide novelty to the classroom structure (freedom), all are designed to be used within a safe and respectful environment (survival), and when the activities are followed by thoughtful class discussions, most can be powerful learning tools (power). Ideas for questions and class discussion topics are included in many of the directions.

The activities in this chapter are organized into four categories: physical games, mind games, drama games, and just plain fun and games. I'd like to emphasize, as I have before in this book, that you are the expert in your subject area and grade level. I've tried to choose activities that lend themselves for use in a wide variety of content areas and range of ages. Please use your judgment in choosing games appropriate for your students, and use your creativity to modify the activities to suit your classroom.

## Physical Games

Physical games are not just for the physical education class; they have a number of benefits for any classroom. First, they provide a welcome change for students from the "sit and git" learning approach they may have experienced in other classes, helping them meet their freedom need. Second, physical games give students opportunities to practice the social skills and character habits you may have discussed in class meetings. Third, they help energize the students, getting blood and oxygen to their brains, preparing them physiologically for more and better learning when they return to their seats. Lastly, they provide many students with another good reason to look forward to your class.

The games in this section require few, if any, materials or equipment. From my years in the classroom, I am well aware of the tight budget that teachers are on. Most of what you would need for these activities are things you already have, can easily find, or pay less than a few dollars for. For example, the first activity requires some toy balloons.

## Boop

This activity will get the students laughing while demonstrating the importance of cooperation and interdependence (Henton, 1996):

1.  Have students form groups of three to five.
2.  Give each group a balloon to blow up.
3.  Have the groups of students form circles, facing inward, hands joined (they won't mind holding hands for this activity).
4.  The object of the game is to keep the balloon up in the air without letting go of hands. They can use any body part to keep the balloon afloat.
5.  For a challenge, give the groups a second balloon, or give them directions like "Heads only," "Elbows only," and so forth.
6.  Afterward, hold a discussion about what made the groups successful. One point that students may bring up is the importance of being flexible and resourceful in our attempts to achieve goals. Also, students may mention that different people may accomplish similar goals in diverse ways.

## Musical Newspapers

For this activity, which will bring your class closer together (in more ways than one), you'll need a tape or CD player and some newspapers (Craigen & Ward, 1994):

1. Place about 15 single newspaper pages (open) on the floor.

2. While the music is playing, students walk around the room. When the music stops, everyone must get onto a newspaper. The object is to get everyone onto the available newspapers.

3. Reduce the number of newspapers each time until you are down to one or two.

4. Encourage students to think of ways to get the whole class on one or two newspapers.

5. A discussion might follow about how we often use more resources than we need and how we might work together to maximize our use of materials and natural resources.

## Balloon Juggle

With students standing in a circle, tell them that you are going to toss a balloon or two into the circle, and their job is to keep them up in the air as best they can. Tell them that if a balloon hits the ground, it's okay to pick it up and put it back into play. Introduce one balloon at a time until you have the same number of balloons as there are students in the game. This is a great energizer and will have the students laughing in no time.

 *Variations:* You might consider placing folded slips of paper in each balloon with discussion topics (see Class Meetings in Chapter 3). After you've introduced all the balloons into the game, stop the action, have students pair up (possibly with someone who has the same color balloon), go somewhere in the room with their partner, pop their balloons and answer the questions inside. You might even want to bring them back to the circle to discuss their questions and answers. This way the activity turns into another great team builder.

*Caution:* Let your neighbors know ahead of time they'll be hearing some loud pops.

## Group Knot

This popular group challenge is guaranteed to create laughter as it develops cooperation (Craigen & Ward, 1994):

1. Have an odd number of students stand in a circle.
2. Ask all to reach out and grab two other hands (you cannot have both hands of the same person, and you cannot have the hand of persons on each side of you).
3. One person must leave her right arm out, and one person must leave his left arm out.
4. Next, direct the group to untangle, without letting go of hands, so that the students are standing in a straight line.
5. The discussion following this game might be about how we often get ourselves into difficult situations, but with patience, cooperation, and good leadership, we can resolve our problems.

## Shoe Scramble

The importance of cooperation will become evident as soon as this game gets started (Craigen & Ward, 1994):

1. Students stand in a circle.
2. Each person in the circle takes off one shoe and places it in the middle.
3. Everyone joins hands.
4. Then, without letting go of hands, each person must pick up a shoe other than their own, find the owner of the shoe and return it to him or her.
5. Hands must be held at all times.
6. Discussion may follow on how (or if) leadership emerged or how important it is to have a process to accomplish certain tasks.

## The Respect Game

This is a great energizer for 10 to 25 players and sends a positive message at the same time. I learned this one from Amanda McCaslin, who said she learned it from her dad, Gary McCaslin, a local pastor. Amanda is one of the students in the Choice Players, a group of students who are trained in Choice Theory and make presentations for students and adults.

1. Students arrange their chairs and sit in a circle, with one student ("*It*") standing in the center holding a Respect Wand (something safe like a rolled up newspaper or a long skinny balloon works well).

2. *It* taps one student on the shoulder with the Respect Wand. All taps in the game should be on the shoulders (no head taps). As *It* taps the student, *It* says, "_____ (*Its name*) *respects* _____ (the name of the tapped student)."

3. The student who was tapped (Student A) stands and says, "_____ (Her own name) *respects* _____ (another student's name—Student B)."

4. *It* must now tap Student B before he stands up, says, "_____ (His name) *respects* _____ (another student—Student C)," and sits down.

5. If *It* is unsuccessful at tapping Student B before he finishes his sentence, *It* stays in the center and play continues.

6. If *It* succeeds in tapping Student B, then Student B and *It* change places.

7. Now, before the former *It* sits down, the new *It* must start the play again by saying, "_____ (Her name) *respects* _____ (any other student)." If the former *It* sits down *before* she finishes," then he goes right back to being *It*.

It takes a little while before students catch on to how the game works. But be patient; before long, you will have kids popping out of their chairs like popcorn, laughing, and respecting each other all over the place.

## The Wave

You've seen this one at football games, but this classroom variation can be hilarious while it teaches students to focus (Craigen & Ward, 1994):

1. Students stand in a circle.
2. The first person in the circle assumes some position of arms, legs, and body and holds it.

3. The second person copies and holds, then the third and so on until all members are holding the shape.
4. The second person in the circle can then try her own shape.
5. Try to move in sequence as quickly as possible to see the wave occur.

 *Variation:* Add a sound to the movement.

## Group Juggle

This adventure-based learning activity is a favorite that helps students understand the concept of interdependence (Rohnke, 1984):

1. Students stand in a circle, with their hands in front of them.
2. The first student calls the name of a student in the circle and tosses him a soft rubber ball.
3. After catching the ball, that player calls the name of another player, makes eye contact with that person, and tosses the ball to her. After throwing the ball, players are instructed to put their hands behind their backs, so it will be clear who has not caught the ball yet.
4. The process continues until everyone has caught the ball. The ball is then tossed back to the first player.
5. Once the pattern is established, the first player tosses out several balls. The challenge is to see how many balls the group can have going at one time.

*Variations:*
• Have a set number of rubber balls (six, for example) and see how fast the group can get them through the pattern once and back to the first player. Try various ways to improve the time.

• Once all the balls are in play, the leader shouts, "Switch" and everyone reverses the order of the pattern. (If you threw me the ball, now I throw it to you.)

Some discussion questions for Group Juggle include the following:

- What was our goal? What did we do that helped us achieve our goal? Is there anything that we did that got in the way of achieving our goal? What could we do to improve the process?
- How is playing this game like life, being in school, being a member of a family, and so forth?
- What attitudes and behaviors help us make this game successful? Where else could those attitudes and behaviors be useful?

## Titles

This energizer helps students understand the idea of broad and narrowly focused questions and learn the skill of sequencing questions logically (Craigen & Ward, 1994):

1. Each student writes the title of a story, book, or movie on a sticky note.
2. Sticky notes are mixed and each student selects one.
3. Without looking at the title, the students place the sticky note they selected on their forehead or back.
4. Students circulate, asking only "Yes" or "No" questions until they identify the title they are wearing.
5. Discussion might follow about the importance of having a logical process to solve problems.

## Towel or Blanket Volleyball

Coordination has a whole new meaning when you rely on a pair or a group (Craigen & Ward, 1994):

1. Divide the class into two teams.
2. Each pair gets a towel or blanket, depending on which you are using.
3. The object of the game is to catch and throw the volleyball over the net with the towel or blanket only. No hands or feet.
4. Discussion might follow about how leadership emerges or the importance of cooperation.

## Circle the Circle

This is a great energizer and icebreaker that will encourage students to encourage one another. Have the class form a hand-in-hand circle. Place two large Hula Hoops between two people (resting on their clasped hands). See how quickly the group can cause each of the hoops to travel around the circle (over people) in opposite directions without anyone letting go of hands. The hoops end at the same place they started. Discussion might follow. If you ask, "Who won?", it takes a moment for them to realize that the entire group has been working as a team. When that is the case, everyone wins (Rohnke, 1984).

## Willow in the Wind

This activity is a great way to build communication and support (literally) among classmates (Henton, 1996):

1. Ten to 15 students stand shoulder-to-shoulder in a circle. One person (the faller) stands in the center, rigid, with arms folded across his chest. The spotters hold a spotting position (one foot slightly in front of the other, hands raised to shoulder height).

2. The group establishes a communication sequence:

   > FALLER: "Are you ready to catch?"
   > SPOTTERS: "Ready."
   > FALLER: "I'm ready to fall."
   > SPOTTERS: "Fall away."

3. Remaining rigid, the faller leans slowly in any direction, maintaining a straight, stiff body and locked knees.

4. Before he moves very far, the circle people redirect the faller and begin to move him around the circle, passing the faller from spotter to spotter in a very gentle fashion, like a "willow in the wind."

5. The fall, catch, nudge sequence continues in a gentle fashion until it becomes obvious that the faller is relaxing (but remaining rigid) and the spotters have gained confidence in their ability to work together effectively.

6. The group guides the faller to stand up in the center of the circle until he regains his balance.

7. Change people in the center until everyone who wants to has had a chance to be the faller.

8. Following the activity, hold a discussion about what made this activity successful (physical and emotional safety, trust, reliability, clear communication, responsibility, etc.). Discuss other situations where those characteristics would be helpful.

## Mind Games

Many students enjoy mental play as much as physical play. Mental games benefit kids, helping them to hone their analytic skills and creativity, and to learn to think "outside the box." There are benefits for teachers as well: mental games take no extra space, require only materials that are already in the classroom, and demonstrate to kids that thinking can be lots of fun. The games in this section can be used in a variety of ways: Some teachers have a brainteaser of the day. Others use them as a transition activity between two subjects or before or after lunch or physical education class. Still others use mental games as an integral part of a learning unit—engaging students in a new unit or extending their knowledge and skills later on. Maybe you'll use them in all of the ways described or in a totally different way. However you use them, you will be glad you did when you hear the laughter (sometimes the groans) and see the smiles (and furrowed foreheads) of your students.

### Sequences

Create sequences that have a logical pattern that is not immediately obvious, and have students explain the sequence or predict the next item in the sequence. Here are a couple of good examples (Rohnke, 1996):

1. What is the pattern that makes the following number sequence logical?

   **8 5 4 9 1 7 6 3 2 0**

(Answer: The numbers are in alphabetical order!)

2. What is the next letter in this sequence? (Hint: To reach the end of this letter line will take more time than you've got.)

O T T F F S S

(Answer: The next letter is E and the sequence is infinite. These letters are in numerical order [One, Two, Three . . . ].)

3. Discussion might follow on how we sometimes jump to conclusions or see things as random occurrences. But if we look a little more closely, we can detect a pattern.

What other sequences can you come up with to boggle your students' minds?

## Bugs in My Cup

This game, discussed in Rohnke (1996), will be one your students are sure to take home to try on their families. Hold a cup in your hands and ask an attentive group, "How many bugs are there in this cup?" The answer, of course, is eight. Only a lucky or very perceptive student will come up with the right answer. So when you say, "How many bugs was that?" and the answer is five, you can be sure they are lucky or that they understand about *bug numbers*. Finally, when you ask, "How many?" and excited voices answer in unison, "Two," you know that the majority has got it. (Answer: How many words were in each question above? That's the number of bugs in the cup.) Here are some ways of asking the question:

- How many bugs are there in this cup that I'm holding? (11)
- How many bugs are there in this cup right here? (10)
- How many bugs are there in this cup? (8)
- How many are there in here? (6)
- How many bugs now? (4)
- How many bugs? (3)

You get the idea! Discussion might follow on the importance of listening carefully and thinking outside the box.

## Initials and Hobbies

This activity requires the students to use a little creativity with their initials. Sitting in a circle, students concentrate on the initials of their first and last name. The challenge is for them to come up with an imaginary hobby with the same set of initials. A short discussion preceding the activity about what is appropriate might be in order (Scher & Verrall, 1992). Here are a few examples:

- Michelle Smith: Marvelous Singing
- Kim Taylforth: Kissing Teddy Bears
- Robert Sullo: Racing Snails
- Jon Erwin: Jello Eating
- Bob Romano: Blasting Rap

## Dictionary Game

For this verbally creative game, you need only a dictionary, paper, pens, and a chalkboard:

1. On slips of paper, have students write invented definitions for words chosen by the teacher. (The teacher checks to see if anyone knows the correct definition.)
2. The teacher collects the slips of paper, adding the correct definition, and shuffles them.
3. In pairs or small groups, have the students choose the definition they think is the correct one.
4. Teams get points for choosing correct definitions. Individual students get points for fooling others into choosing their definitions.

## Restructuring Words

This is another verbal challenge that can be used to teach cooperative groups how to work effectively together (Craigen & Ward, 1994):

1. Present students in cooperative groups with a fairly long multisyllabic word.

2. Challenge the groups to find as many small words as they can within the larger word.

3. Letters may be rearranged.

4. Announce the time limit.

5. Post the total number of words the class came up with. Try to beat the number next time.

6. Discussion might follow on the importance of being skilled at taking things apart (analysis) and putting them back together in a new way (synthesis).

## Math Mind Games

You might present a math puzzler at the beginning of class to get the students engaged while you prepare to teach. Students might work independently or with a partner to figure out the answers to the following:

1. If you have a million dollars and give a hundred dollars away each day, how long will it be before you are broke? (Almost 28 years)

2. How old would you be if you lived a million days? (Almost 2,740 years old)

3. If you live to be 90 years old, approximately how many days will you have lived? (About 32,850 days)

4. If we are in class 180 days this year, and there are 42 minutes in each class, how many minutes will we be spending together? (7,560 minutes) Hours? (126 hours) Days? (5.25 full days)

5. If you always eat three meals a day, how many meals will you have eaten if you live to be 100? (109,500 meals)

6. Find all the combinations of coins that will make 50 cents. (4 nickels and 30 pennies; 2 nickels, 25 pennies, and 2 dimes; 1 nickel, 2 dimes, and 1 quarter; and so on.)

7. If you don't have a ruler or tape measure, what other means could you use to measure the height of your desk? The dimensions of your science book? Your own height? (Use a body part, like the length of your index figure or the width of your hand. Or, use another object, like a dollar bill—which is exactly 6 inches long—or a pencil.)

## Acronyms and Initialisms

This activity will shed new light on "words" that your students hear every day. But they aren't words at all; they're acronyms or initialisms. For example, most people know what a *laser* is, but don't realize that the letters of the acronym stand for *Light Amplification Serialized Emission Radiation*, or that the initialism *4-H* stands for *Head, Heart, Hands, and Health*. "People are fascinated by what they don't know about what they think they should know" (Rohnke, 1996).

Here is how this game works: Print up a list of the following acronyms and initialisms and hand them out to students in groups of three or four. Have the groups try to come up with as many correct answers as possible. Be liberal with what is considered correct. (This is a great way to introduce brainstorming or cooperative group work.) Then watch the lights go on and hear the laughter when you give them the correct answers. Following are some acronyms and initialisms and their meanings:

- ACLU—American Civil Liberties Union
- ACRONYM—A Contrived Reduction of Nomenclature Yielding Mnemonics
- AFL-CIO—American Federation of Labor & Congress of Industrial Organizations
- AWACS—Airborne Warning and Control System
- BIONICS—Biology & Electronics
- BMX—Bicycle Motocross
- CAR-RT—Carrier Route
- CD-ROM—Compact Disc, Read Only Memory
- CNN—Cable News Network
- DDT—Dichlorodiphenyltrichloroethane
- ESPN—Entertainment & Sports Programming Network
- FIAT—Fabricana Italiana Automobile Tornino
- GAR—Grand Army of the Republic
- GIGO—Garbage In, Garbage Out (Computer jargon)
- GMT—Greenwich Mean Time
- GOP—Grand Old Party
- GPA—Grade Point Average
- HMO—Health Maintenance Organization

- ISSN—International Standard Serial Number
- MAFIA—Morte Alla Francia Italia Aneia (Death to the French is Italy's Cry)
- MAYDAY—m'aidez (French for "Help me.")
- M&M's—first letters of the last names of Forrest Mars and Bruce Murrie
- MOPED—Motorized Pedal Cycle
- NASDAQ—National Association of Securities Dealers Automated Quotations
- POETS—Phooey on Everything: Tomorrow's Saturday
- PSAT—Preliminary Scholastic Aptitude Test
- Q.T.—Quiet (as, "on the q.t.")
- RADAR—Radio Detecting and Ranging
- RIF—Reduction in Force
- SAHAND—Society Against Having a Nice Day ☺
- SAM—Surface to Air Missile
- SCUBA—Self-Contained Underwater Breathing Apparatus
- SIDS—Sudden Infant Death Syndrome
- SNAG—Sensitive New Age Guy
- SPAM—Spiced Ham
- TWIMC—To Whom It May Concern
- USO—United Service Organization
- VCR—Videocassette Recorder
- YUPPIE—Young Urban Professional
- ZIP—Zone Improvement Program

Discussion might follow on why we have acronyms. Students might be encouraged to come up with some acronyms and initialisms that would be useful for them.

### What Was That You Said?

This is a great game to boost your students' vocabulary. This mental exercise is for those who already know how to use a dictionary. Present the following complicated phrases to your students and ask them to translate them into well-known sayings or phrases (Craigen & Ward, 1994):

1. Scintillate, scintillate, asteroid minikin.

2. Members of an avian species of identical plumage congregate.

3. It is fruitless to become lachrymose over precipitately departed lacteal fluid.

4. It is fruitless to attempt to indoctrinate a superannuated canine with innovative maneuvers.

5. Where there are visible vapors having their prevalence in ignited carbonaceous materials, there is conflagration.

6. Neophyte's serendipity.

7. Exclusive dedication to necessitous chores without interlude of hedonist diversion renders John an unresponsive fellow.

8. A plethora of individuals with expertise in culinary techniques vitiates the potable concoction produced by steeping certain comestibles.

9. Missiles of ligneous or petrous consistency have the potential of fracturing my caseous structure, but appellations will eternally remain innocuous.

10. A revolving lithic conglomerate accumulates no congeries of a small green bryophytic plant.

These are the translations of the phrases:

1. Twinkle, twinkle, little star.
2. Birds of a feather flock together.
3. Don't cry over spilled milk.
4. Don't try to teach an old dog new tricks.
5. Where there is smoke, there is fire.
6. Beginner's luck.
7. All work and no play makes John a dull boy.
8. Too many cooks spoil the broth.
9. Sticks and stones will break my bones, but names can never hurt me.
10. A rolling stone gathers no moss.

Your students' parents will be scratching their heads when their kids ask them to pass the "lacteal fluid" at the dinner table, or ask "Hey, Mom, when are we going to engage in hedonist diversion this weekend?" You might engage the students in translating well-known teenage or street slang into sophisticated phrases.

### Lateral Thinking Puzzles

Lateral Thinking Puzzles are designed to get students to think "outside the box," to be logical and imaginative at the same time. The great thing about Lateral Thinking Puzzles is that they are great brain exercises and lots of fun at the same time. These can be done independently, but are best solved in pairs or cooperative groups. It is best if one person who knows the solution answers questions posed by others in the group. The questions should be developed so that they can be answered by a "yes," "no," or "irrelevant" response. These puzzles all come from Paul Sloane and Des MacHale in *Great Lateral Thinking Puzzles* (1994), but there are many other Lateral Thinking Puzzle resources available. Here are a few I liked:

- *A Fishy Tale*. A woman had a pet goldfish that she loved dearly. One day she noticed that it was swimming feebly in its bowl and looked very unwell. She rushed to the vet with her prized pet and he told her to come back in an hour. When she returned, she found the goldfish swimming strongly and looking healthy again. How had the vet managed this?

  (Answer: The vet could see that the goldfish was dying of old age, so to spare the old lady's feelings, he dashed out and bought a young but identical fish, and disposed of the old one.)

- *Sheepish Behavior*. On a cold winter's day, drivers found that sheep from the fields nearby kept coming onto the road. There was no snow and the road was not warmer than the fields, but whenever the sheep were ushered back to the fields they quickly returned to the road. Why?

  (Answer: The sheep liked to lick the salt off the road that was put there to keep the road from freezing.)

- *Grandmother's Letter.* A boy at a British boarding school ran out of money, so he wrote to his grandmother asking for a small contribution. She responded with a letter containing a lecture on the evils of extravagance but containing no money of any kind. Nevertheless, the boy was very pleased. Why?

  (Answer: The boy's grandmother was Queen Victoria. In this true incident, the boy sold the letter for five pounds sterling [more than $20 in those days].)

- A *Curious Place.* If you liked this place, you'd rather stay for a day than a year, but if you hated it, you would rather stay for a year than a day. Why?

  (Answer: The place is Venus, where a day is longer than a year. Venus takes 225 Earth days to revolve around the sun, but it takes 243 Earth days to revolve on its axis. This would be a great puzzle to help students understand the concepts of days and years and how the 24-hour day and 365-day year came about.)

- *The Follower.* A woman who was driving alone pulled into a filling station and bought some gasoline. As she drove off she noticed a stranger following her. She tried to shake him off by turning, accelerating, slowing down, and so forth. Finally, she turned into a police station, but was shocked to see him follow her in. He was not a policeman, and there were no mechanical faults with her car. Why did he follow her?

  (Answer: He had seen a man hide in the back of the woman's car as she paid at the gas station. He followed her to warn her and was pleased to see her pull into the police station.)

## WALLY Test Questions

The World Association for Laughing, Learning, and Youth (WALLY) designed these questions to trick and frustrate you, but also to make you laugh. These are to be answered quickly, so tell your students they have no more than 10 seconds to write down their individual responses (Sloane & MacHale, 1994):

1. What is twice the half of 1¼ ?
2. If two peacocks lay two eggs in two days, how many eggs can one peacock lay in four days?
3. How many cubic feet of earth are there in a hole measuring 3-feet-wide by 4-feet-long by 5-feet-deep?
4. Do you know how long cows should be milked?
5. Where was Cleopatra's temple?
6. In what month do Americans eat the least?
7. How many marbles can you put in an empty bag?
8. The grocer stands 6 feet tall, has a 46-inch chest, and wears size 12 shoes. What do you think he weighs?
9. If a duck comes paddling down the Nile, where would it have come from?
10. What would you call a person who does not have all his fingers on one hand?

Here are the answers (get ready to hear groans and growls):

1. 1¼.
2. Peacocks don't lay eggs; peahens do.
3. There is no earth in a hole.
4. The same way as short cows.
5. On the side of her head.
6. February: it has the fewest days.
7. One. After that, it's not empty.
8. Fruit and vegetables.
9. An egg.
10. Normal. Your fingers should be spread equally over two hands.

## Drama Games

If you remember your childhood, chances are that some of your favorite pastimes included games of imagination and role-playing, "let's pretend" games. You might have used action figures or dolls that you made talk and interact, or you might have pretended to be a mommy, a cowboy, a soldier, or even a teacher. As children, our imaginary world, the seat of our creativity, is active and alive. As we grow older and the demands of daily life take their toll, our imagination begins to fade. Drama games can help exercise the imagination, and thus help retain the creative potential we had as children. Drama games in the classroom not only enhance students' creativity, they have other benefits as well. Drama games develop skills that students need to be successful in many other areas of their lives: concentration, focus, self-control, spontaneity, and confidence. Further, many drama games improve students' communication skills: listening, self-expression, articulation, and so on. And finally, drama games give students a chance to move, to interact, and to enjoy the two kinds of freedom (*freedom to* and *freedom from*) that were discussed in the previous chapter. Using drama games in your classroom will have your students clamoring to get in instead of out of your classroom.

## Games for Verbal Expression

**Tongue Twisters.** This verbal game provides good exercise for clear articulation and can be a good transition between classroom activities. They also help develop focus and concentration. Here are some good ones:

- Mixed biscuits.
- Unique New York.
- Sly Sam sips Sally's soup.
- Six sleek swans swam swiftly southward.
- Rubber baby buggy bumpers.
- If a good cook could cook cuckoos, how many cuckoos could a good cook cook, if a good cook could cook cuckoos?
- Bed spreaders spread beds/But bread spreaders spread bread.
- Miss Smith dismisseth us.
- For sheep soup, shoot sheep.
- If you notice this notice, you'll notice this notice is not worth noticing.
- Super thick sticky tape.
- Sally's selfish selling shellfish, so Sally's shellfish seldom sell.

Discussion might follow on the importance of clear enunciation.

**Quacking Up.** Movement, sound, and humor combine to create an energizing warm-up that will have everyone laughing and bonding in minutes:

1. Give each student a card with the name of an animal on it or whisper to each student the name of an animal. Choose animals whose sounds are easy to imitate (cows, dogs, wolves, pigs, etc.).

2. Have the class stand in a circle.

3. Ask them to close their eyes, and tell them when you say, "Go!" they are to make their animal sound and see how many others of their kind they can find and stand together. Tell them they must rely on their sense of hearing to find all the lost sheep, cows, or wolves. (Loomans and Kolberg, 1993)

*Variation:* You might use this to form cooperative learning teams. Another variation is to have students pick their own animals and see how many other students picked the same animal after two minutes.

**One Minute Please.** In this game, a student's name is picked from a hat. That student sits in a "hot seat" and picks a 3" x 5" card from a deck the teacher has prepared. On the card is a subject that the student must talk about for one whole minute. The topics can be anything: sports, boys, girls, television, dancing, hamburgers, commercials, holidays, parents, parties, music, and so on. This activity provides a great opportunity to discuss the importance of a good vocabulary, being able to think on your feet, and good presentation skills (Scher & Verrall, 1992).

**Pet Peeves.** In this variation on One Minute Please, students choose something that annoys them way out of proportion to its importance and sound off about it on the hot seat for a minimum of one minute. It might be a certain television commercial, school hot dogs, food with strange sounding ingredients, gum chewing, or their own middle name. This activity will help students understand the importance of specific examples and vivid language.

*Caution:* You might remind students not to choose a person or any particular category of people. There are plenty of other things to complain about.

**Peas and Carrots.** Start out by having students choose a card with an emotion or characteristic written on it. Their challenge is to convey that emotion or characteristic using only the words "peas and carrots." They may repeat the phrase as many times as they'd like and use facial expressions and gestures for emphasis and added meaning. Emotional states or characteristics include being angry, sad, cruel, silly, tired, bubbly, confused, irritated, pushy, shy, enthused, old, nervous, intelligent, scared, and bossy. After each performance, the audience guesses what emotion or characteristic the student was trying to convey. A discussion might follow about how much meaning is conveyed in everyday communication through tone of voice and nonverbal cues.

## Games for Physical Expression

**Walk This Way.** Students stand in a circle, each person a couple of paces behind the person in front of her, and begin walking around and around the circle. The leader (teacher) calls out, "Walk as if _____," filling in the blank with one of the descriptors below. For example, you might say, "Walk as if you weighed 2000 pounds!" For the next few moments, everyone pantomimes walking as if they weighed a ton. The leader then shouts out "Walk as if _____," filling the blank with another descriptor. The leader may ask students to show different actions, feelings, sensations, perceptions or thoughts. The leader might ask students to walk as if they were

- In terrible pain,
- Swimming through gelatin,
- On the moon,
- On a hot sidewalk with bare feet,
- Getting yelled at by a teacher,
- Wading through deep mud,
- Angry,

- Cold,
- Ice-skating,
- Scared of their own shadows,
- Walking into a surprise party,
- Trudging through the Sahara Desert, or
- Exhausted.

**Have a Seat.** In this game, a chair is placed in the middle of the room. The teacher chooses a student to sit in the seat. As the student approaches the seat, the teacher tells the student, "It's a burning *hot* seat." The student sits down on it and "Yow," he jumps up and stumbles back to his place, rubbing his burned behind as he goes. This student chooses another student and the game continues with a variety of different kinds of seats. Students who have difficulty thinking how to sit in a certain kind of seat may ask a classmate for a suggestion, and then try it on their own. Some possibilities for seats include

- A chair with a tack on it,
- A chair that has been freshly painted,
- A throne,
- The electric chair,
- A slippery seat,
- A smelly seat,
- A seat with someone already in it,
- A seat with itching powder on it,
- A seat next to someone you love, and
- A seat next to someone you don't like.

**Musical Statues.** This game begins when the teacher plays a dance tune. When the music stops, everyone freezes absolutely still, like statues. Anyone who moves is out. The judging becomes stricter until only one person is left. A variation of this is called Freeze and Justify. When the music stops, everyone freezes in whatever position they were in when the music stopped. The teacher taps people at random and they immediately pantomime some everyday action that would justify being in the position they were frozen in (Scher & Verral, 1992, p. 23).

**Greetings.** Some people shake hands when they meet. Others give each other a "high five." In some cultures people kiss each other on either cheek. In this game, the students are paired up and challenged to work out a new way of greeting each other. After 5 or 10 minutes, to the accompaniment of lively music, pairs are invited to demonstrate to the teacher and the class their new greeting. They might see each other, hop three times, and lightly tug on each other's ear. Or they might see each other and leapfrog. Maybe your students will start a new trend!

## Improvisation Games

The television show "Who's Line Is It Anyway" has helped popularize the art of improvisation. In the popular television show, four comedians are presented with a variety of prompts and situations and are awarded points based on how humorously they ad-lib a comedy sketch. Playing some improvisation games in class will give your students a chance to practice their spontaneity and their ability to focus and concentrate under pressure. It also might provide topics for writing assignments.

**Three Props on a Box.** The teacher selects three props (perhaps a ball, a newspaper, and an iron) out of a prop bag and places them on a box. A student selected at random has to come up and tell a story that involves all three props. The more incongruous the props, the more fun and challenging the game is for everyone.

**World's Worst.** This game begins with the students sitting in a circle. Hand each student a card with the name of a profession or hobby on it. The students' challenge is to come to the center of the circle and demonstrate what the World's Worst _____ would look and sound like. This will take some modeling and guided practice. The first few times you do this, you might give out the cards and provide the students with some time to think and prepare. Later on, you could just select a student, hand her a card, and let her improvise. Some possible World's Worsts include the following:

- Server at a restaurant
- Car mechanic
- Motivational speaker

- Singer
- Golfer
- Actor
- Teacher
- Soccer player
- Babysitter
- Rap artist
- Hunter
- Dentist
- Secretary
- Bus driver

**Pick-a-Prop.** Individually, in pairs, or in a small group, students choose an item from a props table and improvise a situation revolving around that prop. For example, a student might choose a handheld mirror and improvise a scene in which he discovers a "zit" on his forehead just minutes before he is to go out for the first time with a special girl (Scher & Verrall, 1992).

**First Lines.** Each pair of students is handed a card with the first line to an improvised skit on it, and they take it from there. This is a real challenge for beginners. Let the action continue until you determine they need to be rescued. It may be after one line or it may go up to three minutes. You might use a gentle signal like a bell or a referee's "time-out" signal to indicate the end. Some possible first lines include

- "Why did you tell on me?"
- "Can you keep a secret?"
- "I've told you before; the answer is *no!*"
- "Whatever made you do that?"
- "It's just not fair!"
- "I've got an apology to make."
- "What a waste of money!"
- "Dad's really mad at you."
- "Why are you always in such a bad mood?"
- "It's just like you to ruin everything."
- "Look, you've got to trust me just this once."
- "Guess what happened to Ashley."

- "What did you just say to me?"
- "You don't own me!"
- "Why can't you see it from my point of view?"
- "You mean this isn't just a cold?"
- "You are not old enough."
- "When are you going to stop that?"
- "How can you be such a liar?"
- "My dog just died."
- "If you don't mind me saying so, you need to go on a diet."
- "I feel sorry for you."
- "I saw what you did last night."
- "You've been talking about me behind my back, haven't you?"
- "Excuse me, I hope you don't think I'm being nosy."
- "You're just jealous!"
- "That is disgusting!"
- "Look, I've got to get something off my chest."
- "I just got in an accident with Mom's car."

## Just Plain Fun and Games

The following activities are ways of having fun in the classroom that don't fit into any of the previous categories but are too good to omit.

### Hagoo

First, divide the class into two teams. Each team stands shoulder to shoulder facing the other, about two steps away from each other. A player from one team stands at one end of the gauntlet, and a player from the other team stands at the other end. They stare at each other until one issues the challenge, "Hagoo!" Next, the two players attempt to walk the entire gauntlet with a very stern frown. If either smiles, that person is won over by the other team and goes to the end of that team's line. It's not unusual for both to burst into laughter simultaneously, in which case, each is won over to the other side. The object of the game is to win over all the other team members. Players cannot touch members of the other team, but they can make faces and say whatever (within reason) might get the frowning person to crack a smile (Kagan, 2000).

Hagoo game appears with permission from Kagan Publishing & Professional Development from Spencer Kagan's book, *Silly Sports and Goofy Games*. www.KaganOnline.com

*Notes:* You might want to set a time limit at the beginning of the game, and the team with the most members at the end of the time limit is the winner. Also, you might want to post neutral observers at either end of the gauntlet to judge if someone has cracked a smile. You could follow this game with a discussion about self-control: Do we choose to laugh, cry, blush, or is it beyond our control?

## Who Is the Leader?

This game starts out with the students sitting in a circle in chairs or at desks. One person leaves the room. Another person is chosen to be leader. The leader stays in his place and gestures, makes faces, and fidgets. The rest of the students in the circle follow along with the leader's actions. The student who left the room returns, joins the circle, and tries to guess who the leader is by carefully observing the group (Craigen & Ward, 1994).

This game might be followed with a discussion on leadership: What is a leader? What kinds of leaders are there? What is the difference between a natural leader and one who is in a position of leadership?

## Look Up–Look Down

This game is both fun and short, so it makes a good transition activity. Students stand in a circle shoulder to shoulder. The group is instructed to "Look Down." When the command "Look Up!" is given, all must do so simultaneously, looking directly at the eyes of any other player. If any pair catch themselves looking at each other, they are both out of the game. If a player ends up looking at a player who is looking at someone else, both players remain in the game. The object of the game is to stay in the circle as long as possible. The last remaining player is the winner (Rohnke, 1996).

This game might be followed up with a discussion of the power of eye contact and of all the messages that can be conveyed just through the eyes.

## I'm Going to California

This is an oldie but a goodie. Once again, the game starts with everyone sitting in a circle. Someone begins by saying, "I'm going to California, and when I go, I'm taking _____." The first player fills in the blank with anything: "my very favorite stuffed poodle," "my dear, dear Aunt Nancy," "five tubs of chocolate pudding," and so on. The more unusual students' selections are, the better. Player two goes on, "I'm going to California, and when I go, I'm taking _____." This person repeats what player one said and adds another item of her own. The object of this game is to go all the way around the circle until the first player has to repeat what he and everyone else has already said and add one more item. For a real challenge, try going around the circle two or three times. You'll be amazed at how much your students can remember when they really focus. Discussion might follow this activity on how we remember all these items and how the strategies used in this game might relate to learning and memory in school and other real-life situations.

### What's My Sign?

This game begins with each person standing in a circle making up a hand signal of some sort. One by one, hand signals are displayed as everyone watches. Students hold their hand signals until everybody has had their turn. One person begins the game by showing her signal and someone else's. The person who recognizes his signal flashes his and someone else's. This continues until someone misses seeing her signal. When this happens you can end the game and start over again, or have that person sit out and continue. A variation is to add a sound to the hand signal (Craigen & Ward, 1994).

### Zip Zap Boing

This game helps students learn to focus and concentrate. It begins with students standing or sitting in a circle. One player starts by turning his head sharply to the right, and exclaiming, "*zip!*" with energy and enthusiasm. The player to his right keeps it going, snapping her head to the right and saying "*zip!*" This continues around the circle until a player shouts "*boing!*" as he turns back to the person to his left. This person snaps his head to the left and says, "*zap!*" Now the wave of zaps continues to the left around the group until another player says, "*boing!*" Then it goes back to the right in a new wave of zips. Just remember:

- *Zip*—to the right
- *Zap*—to the left
- *Boing*—change directions

The object of the game is to create a fast continuous flowing sound and movement around the circle. It takes practice to get to that point, but the practice is lots of fun!

 *Note:* You might consider limiting each player to two boings. Unless you limit the number of boings each person can use, some students become boing-happy and slow down the flow of the game.

## Conclusions

If we look in most classrooms in most schools, we will generally see hard-working teachers and fairly compliant students. There are exceptions, but for the most part, kids will do what they see as necessary to pass their classes and move on to the next grade level. These students are motivated by their desire to avoid problems with teachers, administrators, and parents and to keep up with their classmates. Some are even motivated to excel in some areas by an interest in particular subjects. Although the behavior in these classrooms may be satisfactory and the academic performance adequate, most teachers would not describe these students as highly motivated. Generally, students in these traditional classrooms are not behaving or achieving in a way that we would describe as truly quality.

Most teachers, however, want their students to go beyond merely satisfactory or adequate performance. They want to "reach" students, to kindle the flame of learning inside them. They want to create an inspiring classroom. One characteristic of such a classroom is that it is a joyful place (Glasser, 1998). Fun is an essential ingredient in what anyone would call a "joyful place!"

As teachers, we can deliberately weave fun into our daily lesson plans. To create an inspiring classroom, we must get past the paradigm that learning is always hard work, and that hard work must be painful. Fun is both a prerequisite for and a byproduct of quality learning. It's important to give your students and yourself permission to include fun in your classroom on a daily basis.

# Afterword

I AGREE WITH SULLO WHEN HE SAYS, "TEACHING IS THE NOBLEST PROFESSION" (1999, p. 11). But I also believe that it is one of the most difficult. Students are required by law to attend school every day. They often enter your classroom on the first day of school with negative attitudes because they feel coerced to be there or because of some other reason outside your control. Yet, your job is to prepare them for what is not only the most sophisticated society in history, but also the most challenging.

Teachers can rely on the traditional teaching and managing methods, based primarily on external control psychology (rewards and punishment). But if those methods work at all, it is only in the short term. We also know that using external control erodes trust in the classroom—an essential part to student learning and performance. As renowned child psychologist Virginia M. Axline wrote as long ago as 1947:

> A teacher is more than a dispenser of facts and a tester of accumulated knowledge. It is not enough to hear lessons recited and to "maintain order" in a classroom. Rather, it is the obligation of the teacher to develop sufficient insight and understanding and interest in the human beings that come before her so that they will all know not only subject matter, but themselves and others a little better. (1947, p. 152)

If we truly care about helping our students gain the essential skills to succeed in the 21st century, we must begin by helping them develop the internal motivation to learn. The first step is to develop a classroom environment that encourages students to meet their basic human needs: to survive, to love and belong, to gain power, to be free, and to have fun. Once students discover that they can meet their needs responsibly in the classroom, they will be more likely to learn and perform well and less likely to attempt to act in irresponsible, disruptive ways. Furthermore, once they discover that learning has intrinsic value, chances are good that they will continue to want to learn for the rest of their lives. Whether you use this book as a toolbox of strategies to enhance what you are already doing, or you just use the Unit Guide, the key to success is being intentional about what you do in the classroom. It's a matter of creating a classroom environment by chance or developing the classroom of choice. By intentionally creating the conditions for students to meet their internal needs, you will enjoy getting up in the morning and coming to a classroom where the students and teacher will respectively, as Chaucer put it, "gladly . . . lerne and gladly teche" (*The Canterbury Tales*, l. 308).

# Unit Planning Guide

# Planning a Classroom of Choice: The *I*-Five Approach

DOZENS OF UNIT PLANNING MODELS ARE AVAILABLE: MCCARTHY'S *4MAT*, ASCD and McREL's *Dimensions of Learning* program, and models based on the work of Madeline C. Hunter, to name a few. Many school districts require teachers to use a particular unit and lesson plan format. Although many unit plans recognize the importance of a positive learning environment, none specifically address the five basic needs. If we want to create the conditions for our students to be intrinsically motivated to do quality schoolwork and behave responsibly, it is essential to begin by being intentional about it right from the beginning, in the planning stages. The unit planning model explained in this chapter, the *I*-Five Model, is one that can be easily superimposed on or adapted to fit any unit plan that you are currently using. It can also stand on its own.

## The Human Learning Cycle

The unit plan in this chapter is a simple, adaptable model of the human learning cycle modified to appeal to the five basic needs that provide the foundation for intrinsic motivation. Because it is based on widely accepted ideas regarding the human learning cycle, this model can be used in conjunction with any other good unit or lesson plan format. The human learning-teaching cycle can be seen to have four phases:

*I*-1. *The Introduction Phase.* The goals of this phase are the arousal of interest and positive feelings about the upcoming learning experience through

- Providing clear, meaningful goals.
- Asking essential questions.

- Explaining and discussing learner benefits.
- Raising curiosity.
- Creating a needs-satisfying learning environment.
- Removing learning barriers.
- Getting people active from the start.

I-2. *The Instruction Phase.* The goal of this phase is to help learners interact with new learning material most effectively through

- Activating prior knowledge.
- Pretesting and knowledge sharing.
- Employing a variety of methods of presenting new knowledge and skills.
- Involving the whole brain and whole body.
- Using interactive presentations.
- Appealing to the five basic human needs.

I-3. *The Integration Phase.* The goal of this phase is to help students integrate their new knowledge and skills through

- Using needs-satisfying learner processing activities.
- Providing skill-building practice.
- Providing opportunities for students to write, listen, and speak about the learning.
- Employing cooperative and collaborative teaching and reviewing activities.
- Giving informed, useful, and timely feedback.
- Playing learning games.
- Informally assessing student progress.

I-4. *The Implementation Phase.* The goal of this phase is to help students demonstrate their new knowledge and skills by applying and extending what they have learned in meaningful ways through

- Using authentic, performance-based assessment that is aligned with learning goals.
- Teaching and using self-assessment with students.

- Providing meaningful concurrent assessment.
- Ongoing support and coaching.
- Reteaching and re-evaluating if necessary.
- Employing real-world applications, whenever possible.

In each of these phases, students' basic needs can easily be addressed. It is not absolutely necessary that you have strategies to meet each need in each quadrant of the learning cycle. Many of the strategies in the book meet more than one need. For example, some of the cooperative learning activities that help students meet their need for love and belonging (Chapter 3) also help students meet their need for power and achievement (Chapters 4 and 5), give them a sense of *freedom from* "chalk-and-talk" teaching (Chapter 6), and are fun (Chapter 7). The important thing is to find a balance that works for your students. It may take some experimentation, but you will know when you've found it. I'd recommend starting with a fairly equal balance and make adjustments according to your observations of what strategies work best with your students. You might even consider keeping a journal.

### Involvement: The Fifth *I*

The human learning cycle does not exist within a vacuum. The fifth *I*, involvement, refers to the relationships that surround the student as he is introduced to, gains, integrates, and implements his new knowledge or skills (see Figure UPG.1). As we learned in Chapter 1, trusting relationships are essential to quality learning. Planning for involvement is a way of enhancing trusting relationships.

There are two general categories of involvement: personal involvement and role involvement. *Personal involvement* refers to the positive, accepting relationships that teachers encourage between and among themselves and their students. *Role involvement* refers to the clarification of responsibilities within the learning environment. As a learner, I need both kinds of involvement to experience a high degree of trust as I face the risks inherent in undertaking a new learning task. I need to know that I am accepted by my teacher and my peers. I also need to have a clear understanding of what I may and may not expect from my teacher as well as what my own responsibilities are in the learning process.

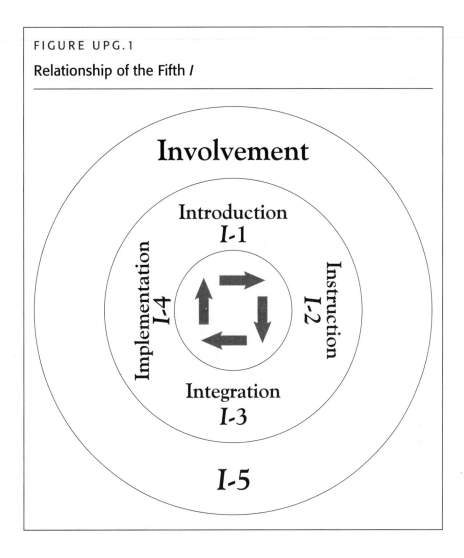

**FIGURE UPG.1**

**Relationship of the Fifth *I***

Involvement

Introduction
*I*-1

Implementation
*I*-4

Instruction
*I*-2

Integration
*I*-3

*I*-5

The involvement component of the *I*-Five Planning Process is something that I recommend focusing on from the beginning of the school year. Strategies like the Class Constitution and team-building activities go a long way toward creating involvement. However, involvement is an ongoing process; you don't just "set it and forget it" like the Ronco rotisserie. You can use many strategies throughout the year to build and maintain the personal and role involvement you develop in the first few weeks of school.

Although most of the strategies explained in this book are designed for use within particular learning units, others are intended to develop involvement. Some are designed for use at the beginning of the year to help set clear expectations, clarify roles, and develop a warm, supportive classroom environment. Still other strategies might be used on an ongoing basis as needs-satisfying procedures and routines to help the classroom run smoothly and to maintain the involvement developed at the beginning of the year.

In Appendix A, strategies that lend themselves to developing involvement are identified under the column marked *I-5*. Appendix B provides a template to list the specific practices you plan to use to accomplish these goals. I recommend addressing all five of the basic human needs as you plan involvement strategies.

## The Unit Planning Guide

Before planning the strategies you will include in your plans, it is essential to identify what you want your students to know and be able to do by the end of a unit of study. List those goals in the Learning Objectives box. The Essential Questions box asks you to come up with a few (between one and three) questions that should be the general guiding questions throughout the learning unit, questions that all students should be able to answer by the end. Many unit plans ask you to identify these objectives and questions. Others go further, asking you to identify the main concept that the unit will focus on. If your district or school unit plan already addresses these components, there is no need to rewrite them on this plan. If not, however, taking the time to identify intentionally the knowledge and skills you want your students to learn is essential to quality teaching and learning. Doing this enables you to select and align effective teaching strategies with your learning goals.

The *I*-Five Unit Plan template in Appendix C asks the teacher to consider the five basic needs in each of four phases of the learning cycle: Introduction, Instruction, Integration, and Implementation. To assist in planning, Appendix A lists all the strategies explained in the book with recommendations for the phases of the learning cycle they best fit.

# *I*-Five Phase Strategies

All the strategies suggested in this book are listed by the need they address in the classroom. The Xs in the boxes adjacent to each strategy indicate for which phase of the learning cycle that strategy is most appropriate. Some of the strategies can be used in more than one learning phase. Those are indicated by multiple Xs.

The first four boxes represent the following: *I*-1: Introduction, *I*-2: Instruction, *I*-3: Integration, and *I*-4: Implementation. The box marked *I*-5 represents strategies recommended for developing Involvement, either at the beginning of the year or on an ongoing basis throughout the year. A *B* under the *I*-5 column indicates those strategies that are recommended for the beginning of the year. An *O* indicates those recommended for use on an ongoing basis to build or maintain involvement.

## Survival in the Classroom

| Pg | Strategy | I-1 | I-2 | I-3 | I-4 | I-5 |
|----|----------|-----|-----|-----|-----|-----|
| 24 | Water Breaks | | | | | O |
| 25 | Snacks | | | | | O |
| 26 | Breathing or Stretch Breaks | | | | | O |
| 26 | Energizers | X | X | X | | O |
| 26 | Greetings | | | | | O |
| 27 | Positive Posters | | | | | O |
| 27 | Classroom Guidelines for Behavior | | | | | B |
| 29 | Proximity | | | | | O |
| 29 | General Reminder | | | | | O |
| 29 | What Are You Doing? | | | | | O |
| 29 | The Gentle Reminder | | | | | O |
| 29 | The Teacher Look | | | | | O |
| 30 | Impose Consequences | | | | | O |
| 30 | Individual Counseling | | | | | O |
| 34 | Journal Writing or Sponge Activity | | | | | O |

| Pg | Strategy | I-1 | I-2 | I-3 | I-4 | I-5 |
|----|----------|-----|-----|-----|-----|-----|
| 35 | Quiet Signal: Clapping Hands, Wind Chimes, Raise Hands, Lights Out, Sound Effects, Consistent Verbal Message | | | | | O |
| 36 | Procedures for Students Seeking Help: Hand Signal, Toilet Tissue Tube, Index Card, Textbook, Desk Dots, Bookmarks | | | | | O |
| 37 | Procedures for Collecting Student Work: Crates, Across the rows | | | | | O |
| 38 | Teaching Anger/Frustration Management Skills: Behavioral Car, Behavioral Traffic Circle, Deep Breath and Positive Thought, Comfortable Chair | | | | | O |
| 42 | Daily or Weekly Agenda | X | | | | O |
| 43 | Team-Building Activities | X | | | | B,O |
| 43 | Journal Communication | X | | | | O |
| 43 | Music | X | X | X | X | O |
| 44 | Manners | | | | | B,O |

## Love and Belonging in the Classroom

| Pg | Strategy | I-1 | I-2 | I-3 | I-4 | I-5 |
|----|----------|-----|-----|-----|-----|-----|
| 48 | Name Games: Nametags with Symbols, Name Cards, Names with Adjectives, Bumpety-Bump-Bump, Connect-a-Name | | | | | B |
| 50 | Pre-First Day of School Letter | | | | | B |
| 50 | Greet Students at the Door | | | | | B,O |
| 51 | The First-Day Test | | | | | B |
| 52 | Interest Inventory | X | | | | B |
| 52 | Extracurricular Activities | | | | | O |
| 53 | Journals | X | X | X | X | O |
| 53 | Lunch with the Teacher | | | | | O |

## APPENDIX A

| Pg | Strategy | I-1 | I-2 | I-3 | I-4 | I-5 |
|----|----------|-----|-----|-----|-----|-----|
| 56 | Manners 101 | | | | | B,O |
| 58 | Human Scavenger Hunt | X | | X | | B |
| 59 | "Do You Know Your Neighbors?" | | | | | O |
| 60 | People Bingo | X | | X | | B |
| 60 | Toilet Paper Introductions | X | | | | B |
| 62 | Food Discussions | X | | | | B,O |
| 62 | Pairs of Hands | X | | | | B,O |
| 62 | Bag o' Needs | | | | | B |
| 63 | Class Web | X | | | | B |
| 64 | True or False | X | | X | | B,O |
| 64 | Baby, Look at You Now | X | | | | B,O |
| 64 | Line-Ups | X | X | X | | B,O |
| 65 | Corners | X | X | X | | B,O |
| 66 | Personalogies | X | | | | O |
| 66 | Animalogies | X | | | | O |
| 67 | Class Quilt | X | | | | B,O |
| 69 | Mix-Freeze-Pair | X | X | X | | O |
| 70 | Trading Cards | X | | X | | B,O |
| 70 | Uncommon Commonalities | X | | | | O |
| 71 | Theme Days | X | | | | O |
| 71 | Predictions and Perceptions | X | | | | O |
| 72 | Group Résumé | X | | X | | O |
| 73 | Class Mission Statement | | | | | B |
| 76 | Strategies for Pairing Students: Mix-Freeze-Pairs, Opposite Cards, Pacing Partners, Appointment Book Partners, Door Cards | X | X | X | X | O |
| 79 | Inside-Outside Circle | X | X | X | | B,O |
| 79 | Brains Storming | | X | X | | |

| Pg | Strategy | I-1 | I-2 | I-3 | I-4 | I-5 |
|----|----------|-----|-----|-----|-----|-----|
| 81 | Pairs Discuss | | | X | | O |
| 81 | Pick a Card, Any Card | X | X | X | | O |
| 82 | Jigsaw | X | X | X | | O |
| 83 | Graffiti | X | X | X | | O |
| 83 | Formations | X | X | X | X | O |
| 84 | All Hands on Deck | X | X | X | | O |
| 85 | I Have–Who Has | | | X | | O |
| 86 | Inquiring Minds | X | | | | |
| 87 | Team or Pair Projects | | | | X | O |
| 90 | Class Meetings | X | X | X | X | B,O |

## Power in the Classroom: Environment

| Pg | Strategy | I-1 | I-2 | I-3 | I-4 | I-5 |
|----|----------|-----|-----|-----|-----|-----|
| 101 | The Class Constitution | | | | | B,O |
| 105 | The Classroom Needs Circle | | | | | B,O |
| 105 | Student-Chosen Themes | | | | | O |
| 106 | Know-Want-Learned (KWL) | X | X | X | X | |
| 108 | Specific Feedback | | | | | O |
| 108 | Parent Postcards | | | | | O |
| 108 | Celebrations | | | | | O |
| 109 | Peer Recognition | | | | | O |
| 109 | Publish | | | | X | O |
| 110 | Suggestion Box | | | | | O |
| 110 | Kid of the Week | | | | | O |
| 111 | Needs Collage | | | | | B |
| 111 | Class Jobs | | | | | O |
| 112 | Peer Tutors | | | | | O |

APPENDIX A

| Pg | Strategy | I-1 | I-2 | I-3 | I-4 | I-5 |
|----|----------|-----|-----|-----|-----|-----|
| 112 | Peer Mediators | | | | | O |
| 112 | Teach and Tell | | | | X | O |
| 115 | Students of Choice | | | | | B,O |

## Power in the Classroom: Student Achievement

| Pg | Strategy | I-1 | I-2 | I-3 | I-4 | I-5 |
|----|----------|-----|-----|-----|-----|-----|
| 122 | SAVI Teaching Strategies | X | X | X | X | |
| 122 | Cross-Lateral Exercises | X | | | | O |
| 123 | Hot Potato Pretest | X | X | X | | O |
| 123 | Walking Class | X | X | | | O |
| 123 | Walking Pair-Share | | X | X | | O |
| 123 | Skits | | | X | X | O |
| 124 | Model Building | | | X | X | O |
| 124 | Question-and-Answer Shuffle | | | X | X | O |
| 124 | Walk Through the Steps | | X | X | | |
| 124 | Frisbee Review | | X | X | | O |
| 124 | Puzzle Assembly | | X | X | | |
| 124 | In-Class Scavenger Hunt | X | X | X | | O |
| 125 | Balloons Pop Quiz | | X | X | | |
| 125 | Music as Inspiration | X | X | X | X | O |
| 126 | Concert Preview | X | | | | O |
| 126 | Audio Clips | X | X | | | |
| 127 | Storytelling | X | X | | | O |
| 127 | Mnemonics | | X | X | | |
| 127 | Songs | | X | X | | O |
| 127 | Guided Imagery | | X | X | | |
| 128 | Sense Imagery | X | X | X | | |

APPENDIX A

| Pg | Strategy | I-1 | I-2 | I-3 | I-4 | I-5 |
|---|---|---|---|---|---|---|
| 129 | Peripherals | X | X | X | X | O |
| 129 | Model Presentation | | X | | | |
| 129 | Mind Maps | | X | | | |
| 130 | Graphic Organizers | X | X | X | | |
| 130 | Group Mural | | X | X | X | O |
| 130 | Link Strategy | | X | X | | |
| 131 | Rhyming Peg Word | | X | | | |
| 132 | Living Props | | X | X | | |
| 133 | Instructor Role Play | | X | | | |
| 134 | Props to Illustrate Concepts | | X | | | |
| 134 | Information Doodles | | X | X | | |
| 135 | Collaborative Pretest | X | X | | | O |
| 135 | Student-Generated Questions | X | X | | | O |
| 136 | Thematic Integrated Units | | | | | O |
| 137 | Pulse Learning | | | | | O |
| 137 | The Three-Minute Pause | | X | | | |
| 138 | Learning Journals | X | X | X | X | O |
| 139 | Presentation Roulette | | X | | | |
| 139 | Collaborative Definitions | | X | X | | O |
| 139 | Pair Teaching | | X | X | X | O |
| 140 | Alignment | | | | | O |
| 141 | Assessment Choices | | | | X | O |
| 144 | Competence-Based Classroom | | | | X | O |

## Freedom in the Classroom

| Pg | Strategy | I-1 | I-2 | I-3 | I-4 | I-5 |
|---|---|---|---|---|---|---|
| 150 | Novelty | | | | | O |
| 151 | Mastery Learning | | | | X | O |

APPENDIX A

| Pg | Strategy | I-1 | I-2 | I-3 | I-4 | I-5 |
|----|----------|-----|-----|-----|-----|-----|
| 152 | Chill Out Chair | | | | | O |
| 153 | Choice of Seats | X | | | | O |
| 154 | Daily or Weekly Agenda | | | | | O |
| 154 | Choice of Partners or Team Members | X | | | | O |
| 155 | Student-Generated Curriculum | X | | | | O |
| 156 | Order of Learning Units | | | | | O |
| 157 | Choices Within Assignments | | | X | X | |
| 157 | Free-Reading Friday | | | | | O |
| 157 | Free Writing | | | | | O |
| 158 | Choice of Performance Assessment | | | | X | O |
| 158 | Portfolio Choices | | | | X | O |

## Fun in the Classroom

| Pg | Strategy | I-1 | I-2 | I-3 | I-4 | I-5 |
|----|----------|-----|-----|-----|-----|-----|
| 164 | Boop | | | | | O |
| 164 | Musical Newspapers | | | | | O |
| 165 | Balloon Juggle | | | | | O |
| 165 | Group Knot | | | | | O |
| 166 | Shoe Scramble | | | | | O |
| 166 | The Respect Game | | | | | O |
| 167 | The Wave | | | | | O |
| 168 | Group Juggle | | | | | O |
| 169 | Titles | | | X | | O |
| 169 | Towel or Blanket Volleyball | | | | | O |
| 170 | Circle the Circle | | | | | O |
| 170 | Willow in the Wind | | | | | O |
| 171 | Sequences | | | X | | O |
| 172 | Bugs in My Cup | | | | | O |

APPENDIX A

| Pg | Strategy | I-1 | I-2 | I-3 | I-4 | I-5 |
|---|---|---|---|---|---|---|
| 173 | Initials and Hobbies | | | | | O |
| 173 | Dictionary Game | | | | | O |
| 173 | Restructuring Words | | | | | O |
| 174 | Math Mind Games | | | | | O |
| 175 | Acronyms and Initialisms | | | | | O |
| 176 | What Was That You Said? | | | | | O |
| 178 | Lateral Thinking Puzzles | | | | | O |
| 179 | WALLY Test Questions | | | | | O |
| 181 | Tongue Twisters | | | | | O |
| 182 | Quacking Up | | | | | O |
| 182 | One Minute Please | | | | | O |
| 182 | Pet Peeves | | | | | O |
| 183 | Peas and Carrots | | | | | O |
| 183 | Walk This Way | | | | | O |
| 184 | Have a Seat | | | | | O |
| 184 | Musical Statues | | | | | O |
| 185 | Greetings | | | | | O |
| 185 | Three Props on a Box | | | | | O |
| 185 | World's Worst | | | | | O |
| 186 | Pick-a-Prop | | | | | O |
| 186 | First Lines | | | | | O |
| 187 | Hagoo | | | | | O |
| 188 | Who is the Leader? | | | | | O |
| 188 | Look Up–Look Down | | | | | O |
| 188 | I'm Going to California | | | | | O |
| 189 | What's My Sign? | | | | | O |
| 189 | Zip Zap Boing | | | | | O |

# *I*-Five: A Guide for Developing and Maintaining Personal and Role Involvement

**\*Key to Needs:**

Survival - S   Love and Belonging- LB   Power- P   Freedom- FR   Fun – F

| Purpose | Strategies and Page Numbers | Basic Needs Addressed* (Check those that apply.) | | | | |
|---|---|---|---|---|---|---|
| | | S | LB | P | FR | F |
| Developing behavioral guidelines | | | | | | |
| Clarifying roles | | | | | | |
| Creating a sense of community | | | | | | |
| Empowering students | | | | | | |
| Maintaining a needs-satisfying environment: Ongoing procedures and routines | | | | | | |

APPENDIX C

# The *I*-Five Unit Guide

Title of Unit: _____

| Learning Objectives | |
| --- | --- |
| What do you want your students to know and be able to do by the end of this learning unit? | |
| **Essential Questions** | |
| What two or three general questions would you like your students to keep in mind throughout the unit and be able to answer by the end? | |

*Key to Needs:

Survival - S   Love and Belonging- LB   Power- P   Freedom- FR   Fun – F

| Teaching-Managing Strategies | | | | | | |
|---|---|---|---|---|---|---|
| **Introduction** | **Strategies and Page Numbers** | Basic Needs Addressed*<br>(Check those that apply.) | | | | |
| | | S | LB | P | FR | F |
| **Arousing interest & positive feelings through**<br><br>• providing clear, meaningful goals<br><br>• discussing learner benefits<br><br>• raising curiosity<br><br>• creating a needs-satisfying learning environment<br><br>• removing learning barriers<br><br>• getting students active from the start | | | | | | |

APPENDIX C

| Instruction | Strategies and Page Numbers | Basic Needs Addressed* (Check those that apply.) | | | | |
|---|---|---|---|---|---|---|
| | | S | LB | P | FR | F |
| **Helping learners interact with new learning material most effectively through** <br><br> • activating prior knowledge <br><br> • pre-testing and knowledge sharing <br><br> • employing a variety of methods of presenting new knowledge and skills <br><br> • involving the whole brain and whole body <br><br> • using interactive presentations <br><br> • appealing to the five basic human needs | | | | | | |

APPENDIX C

| Integration | Strategies and Page Numbers | Basic Needs Addressed* (Check those that apply.) | | | | |
|---|---|---|---|---|---|---|
| | | S | LB | P | FR | F |
| **Helping students integrate their new knowledge and skills through**<br><br>• using needs-satisfying learner processing activities<br><br>• providing skill-building practice providing<br><br>• opportunities for students to write, listen, and speak about the learning<br><br>• employing cooperative and collaborative<br><br>• teaching and reviewing activities<br><br>• giving informed, useful and timely feedback<br><br>• playing learning games<br><br>• informally assessing student progress | | | | | | |

## APPENDIX C

| Implementation | Strategies and Page Numbers | Basic Needs Addressed* (Check those that apply.) | | | | |
|---|---|---|---|---|---|---|
| | | S | LB | P | FR | F |
| **Helping students demonstrate their new knowledge and skills by applying and extending what they have learned in meaningful ways through** | | | | | | |
| • using authentic assessment that is aligned with learning goals | | | | | | |
| • teaching and using | | | | | | |
| • student self-assessment | | | | | | |
| • providing meaningful concurrent assessment | | | | | | |
| • ongoing support and coaching | | | | | | |
| • reteaching and reevaluating if necessary | | | | | | |
| • employing real-world applications, whenever possible | | | | | | |

# References

Aguayo, R. (1990). *Dr. Deming.* New York: Simon & Schuster, Inc.

Anderson, S. A. (1994). Synthesis of research on mastery learning. Washington, DC: National Educational Association (ERIC Document Reproduction Service No. ED382567).

Axline, V. M. (1947). *Play therapy, the inner dynamics of childhood.* New York: Ballantine Books.

Barton, L. G. (1997). *Quick flip questions for critical thinking.* Dana Point, CA: Edupress, Inc.

Bloom, B. S. (1968). Learning for mastery. *Evaluation Comment (UCLA-CSIEP), 1*(2), 1–12.

Bryk, A. S., & Schneider, B. (2002). *Trust in schools: A core resource for improvement.* New York: Russell Sage Foundation.

Christian, S. G., & Tubesing, N. L. (1997). *Instant icebreakers: 50 powerful catalysts for group interaction and high-impact learning.* Duluth, MN: Whole Person.

Covey, S. R. (1989). *The seven habits of highly effective people.* New York: Simon & Schuster, Inc.

Craigen, J., & Ward, C. (1994). *What's this got to do with anything.* Ajax, ON: Visutronx.

Ellis, A. K., & Fouts, J. T. (1997). *Research on educational innovations.* Larchmont, NY: Eye on Education.

Gardner, H. (1993). *Multiple intelligences: The theory in practice.* New York: HarperCollins Publishers.

Glasser, W. (1969). *Schools without failure.* New York: Harper & Row Publishers, Inc.

Glasser, W. (1984). *Control theory: A new explanation of how we control our lives.* New York: Harper & Row Publishers, Inc.

Glasser, W. (1992). *The quality school: Managing students without coercion.* New York: HarperPerennial.

Glasser, W. (1998). *Choice Theory: A new psychology of personal freedom.* New York: HarperCollins Publishers.

Glasser, W. (2000a). *Counseling with Choice Theory: The new reality therapy*. New York: HarperCollins Publishers.

Glasser, W. (2000b). *Every student can succeed*. Chula Vista, CA: Black Forest Press.

Goldman, D. (1995). *Emotional intelligence*. New York: Bantam Books.

Guskey, T. R. (1997). *Implementing mastery learning*. Belmont, CA: Wadsworth.

Hargis, C. H. (1995). *Curriculum based assessment: A primer*. Springfield, IL: Charles C. Thomas Publisher.

Harmin, M. (1995). *Inspiring discipline*. West Haven, CT: NEA Professional Library.

Harris, D. (2000). *Synergy: Connecting to the power of cooperation*. Salt Lake City, UT: Franklin Covey Company.

Henton, M. (1996). *Adventure in the classroom: Using adventure to strengthen learning and build a community of life-long learners*. Dubuque, IA: Kendall Hunt Publishing Company.

Jensen, E. (1997). *Brain compatible strategies*. Del Mar, CA: Turning Point Publishing.

Jensen, E. (1998). *Teaching with the brain in mind*. Alexandria, VA: Association for Supervision and Curriculum Development.

Johnson, D. W., Johnson, R. T., & Holubec, E. J. (1993). *Circles of learning: Cooperation in the classroom*. Edina, MN: Interaction Book Company.

Kagan, S. (1994). *Cooperative learning*. San Clemente, CA: Kagan Publishing.

Kagan, S. (2000). *Silly sports and goofy games*. San Clemente, CA: Kagan Publishing.

Kohn, A. (1993). *Punished by rewards: The trouble with gold stars, incentive plans, A's, and other bribes*. Boston: Houghton Mifflin.

Kohn, A. (1999). *The schools our children deserve*. Boston: Houghton Mifflin.

Loomans, D. & Kolberg, K. J. (1993). *The laughing classroom: Everyone's guide to teaching with humor and play*. Tirburon, CA: H. J. Kramer.

Marzano, R. J., & Pickering, D. J. (1997). *Dimensions of learning teacher's manual*. 2nd ed. Alexandria, VA: Association for Supervision and Curriculum Development.

McCarthy, B. (1987). *4MAT system: Teaching to learning styles with right-left mode techniques*. Wauconda, IL: About Publishing.

Meier, D. (1999). Accelerated learning course builder. [Multimedia toolkit] Lake Geneva, WI: Center for Accelerated Learning.

Ornish, D. (1998). *Love & survival: The scientific basis for the healing power of intimacy*. New York: HarperCollins.

Rohnke, K. (1984). *Silver bullets: A guide to initiative problems, adventure games, stunts, and trust activities*. Hamilton, MA: Project Adventure; and Dubuque, IA: Kendall/Hunt Publishing Company.

Rohnke, K. (1996). *Funn stuff*. Dubuque, IA: Kendall/Hunt Publishing Company.

Rutherford, P. (1998). *Instruction for all students.* Alexandria, VA: Just ASK Publications.

Scher, A. & Verrall, C. (1992). *200+ ideas for drama.* Portsmouth, NH: Heinemann.

Shaw, V. (1992). *Community building in the classroom.* San Juan Capistrano, CA: Kagan Cooperative Learning.

Silberman, M. L. (1996). *Active learning: 101 strategies to teach any subject.* Boston: Allyn and Bacon.

Sloane, P. & MacHale, D. (1994). *Great lateral thinking puzzles.* New York: Sterling Publishing Company.

Sullo, R. A. (1997). *Inspiring quality in your school: From theory to practice.* West Haven, CT: NEA Professional Library.

Sullo, R. A. (1999). *The inspiring teacher: New beginnings for the 21st century.* West Haven, CT: NEA Professional Library.

Wong, H. K., & Wong, R. T. (1998). *The first days of school: How to be an effective teacher.* Mountain View, CA: Harry K. Wong Publications.

Wubbolding, R. E. (1988). *Using reality theory.* New York: HarperCollins.

# Index

# About the Author

In his 11 years as a middle and senior high school teacher, **Jonathan C. Erwin** taught English and a variety of electives to students in grades 7–12, coached track and cross country, and directed several plays and musicals. From 1996 until 2003, Erwin was a staff development and curriculum specialist with the Board of Cooperative Educational Services (BOCES), serving a three-county region around Elmira, New York. He also has been a faculty member of The William Glasser Institute since 1995, is an adjunct faculty member of Elmira College, and is a part-time professor at Lock Haven University. Erwin is also the founder and director of The Choice Players, a group of students, ages 12 to 19, who learn Choice Theory and teach it to others at local and national conferences and trainings.

Erwin now works as an independent educational consultant based in Corning, New York. For information on training or consulting, visit his Web site at http://www.jonerwin.com, e-mail at jerwin2@stay.rr.com, or call (607) 937-5499.

# Related ASCD Resources

## The Classroom of Choice: Giving Students What They Need and Getting What You Want

At the time of publication, the following ASCD resources were available; for the most up-to-date information about ASCD resources, go to http://www.ascd.org. ASCD stock numbers are noted in parentheses.

### Audio

*Student Motivation: What Do We Know? What Do We Need to Know?* by Bea McGarvey (#204074 audiotape; #504108 CD)

*Motivating Students Who Don't Care* by Allen Mendler (#203128 audiotape; #503221 CD)

*Using Motivation as the Foundation for Renewal in Urban High Schools* by Lorenzo Garcia and Margery Ginsberg (#201141 audiotape)

### Multimedia

*Classroom Management/Positive School Climate Topic Pack* (#198219)

*Classroom Management Professional Inquiry Kit* by Robert Hanson (eight activity folders and a videotape). (#998059)

*Dimensions of Learning Complete Program* (teacher's and trainer's manuals, book, 6 videos, and an additional free video) Educational consultants: Robert J. Marzano and Debra J. Pickering (#614239)

### Networks

Visit the ASCD Web site (http://www.ascd.org) and search for "networks" for information about professional educators who have formed groups around topics like "Invitational Instruction," "Middle Grades," and "Quality Education." Look in the "Network Directory" for current facilitators' addresses and phone numbers.

### Online Resources

Visit ASCD's Web site (www.ascd.org) for the following professional development opportunities:

Education Topic: *School Culture/Climate* (free)

Professional Development Online: *Dimensions of Learning* and *Surviving and Thriving in Your First Year of Teaching*, among others (for a small fee; password protected).

### Print Products

*Activating and Engaging Habits of Mind* by Arthur L. Costa and Bena Kallick (#100033)

*Classroom Management That Works: Research-Based Strategies for Every Teacher* by Robert J. Marzano with Jana S. Marzano and Debra J. Pickering (#103027)

*Connecting with Students* by Allen N. Mendler (#101236)

*Educational Leadership: Building Classroom Relationships* (entire issue, September 2003) Excerpted articles online free; entire issue online and accessible to ASCD members

*Fulfilling the Promise of the Differentiated Classroom: Strategies and Tools for Responsive Teaching* by Carol Ann Tomlinson (#103107)

*The Key Elements of Classroom Management: Managing Time and Space, Student Behavior, and Instructional Strategies* by Joyce MacLeod, Jan Fisher, and Ginny Hoover (#103008)

*Motivating Students and Teachers in an Era of Standards* by Richard Sagor (#103009)

*Schooling for Life: Reclaiming the Essence of Learning* by Jacqueline Grennon Brooks (#101302)

### Videos

*Educating Everybody's Children* (3 videos and facilitator's guide) (#400220)

*How to Design Classroom Management to Enhance Learning* (Tape 16 of the How To Series) (#403114)

*Motivation: The Key to Success in Teaching and Learning* (3 videos and facilitator's guide) (#403344)

*A Visit to a Motivated Classroom* (#403384)

For more information, visit us on the World Wide Web (http://www.ascd.org), send an e-mail message to member@ascd.org, call the ASCD Service Center (1-800-933-ASCD or 703-578-9600, then press 2), send a fax to 703-575-5400, or write to Information Services, ASCD, 1703 N. Beauregard St., Alexandria, VA 22311-1714 USA.